TWAYNE'S WORLD AUTHORS SERIES

A Survey of the World's Literature

Sylvia E. Bowman, Indiana University

GENERAL EDITOR

FRANCE

Maxwell A. Smith, Guerry Professor of French, Emeritus
The University of Chattanooga
Visiting Professor in Modern Languages
The Florida State University

EDITOR

Gustave Flaubert

(TWAS 3)

TWAYNE'S WORLD AUTHORS SERIES (TWAS)

The purpose of TWAS is to survey the major writers
—novelists, dramatists, historians, poets, philosophers,
and critics—of the nations of the world. Among the
national literatures covered are those of Australia,
Canada, China, Eastern Europe, France, Germany,
Greece, India, Italy, Japan, Latin America, New Zea-
land, Poland, Russia, Scandinavia, Spain, and the
African nations, as well as Hebrew, Yiddish, and
Latin Classical literatures. This survey is comple-
mented by Twayne's United States Authors Series
and English Authors Series.

The intent of each volume in these series is to present
a critical-analytical study of the works of the writer;
to include biographical and historical material that
may be necessary for understanding, appreciation,
and critical appraisal of the writer; and to present all
material in clear, concise English—but not to vitiate
the scholarly content of the work by doing so.

Gustave Flaubert

By STRATTON BUCK

University of the South

Twayne Publishers, Inc.   ::   New York

Library of Congress Catalog Card Number: 66–16120

For

EMILY

"ma vieille tendresse"

GUSTAVE FLAUBERT

Preface

THE pages which follow are intended to provide the student and general reader with an introduction to the novels and the correspondence of Gustave Flaubert. I have drawn heavily from Flaubert's letters in an effort to present a picture of his personality, his attitudes, and his esthetic convictions. I have endeavored to present a historical and critical appreciation of each of the works of the writer's maturity. I have attempted to discover the genesis of each of the six novels, to follow the evolution and the composition of the work, to describe the nature and the content of each book, and to offer an estimate of its importance.

No effort has been made to compile a complete biography; the events and vicissitudes of Flaubert's life appear, therefore, only when they are directly related to his writing. It is curious to note, however, the extent to which this author who wished to make posterity believe that he did not exist is present in his work. The discussion is limited to the novels published or about to be published during Flaubert's lifetime. There is only passing mention of the *Juvenilia*, the travel journals, and the dramas.

My indebtedness to the company of Flaubert scholars, past and present, on whose work I have drawn freely, is obvious. If this study provides readers of English with a sound, up-to-date, and readable evaluation of the career and work of Flaubert, it will have achieved its purpose.

I am grateful for the confidence, encouragement, and suggestions of Dr. Sylvia Bowman, the general editor of Twayne's World Authors Series, and of my good friend, Dr. Maxwell A. Smith, the French editor of these publications. Thanks are due to the Viking Press and the Editions du Seuil for permission to quote from Lionel Trilling's *The Opposing Self* and from Jean-Pierre Richard's *Littérature et Sensation,* and to the editors of the *Sewanee Review* for authorization to reproduce portions of my article "For Emma Bovary." Mrs. Kenneth Ware has been more than helpful in the preparation of the typescript.

STRATTON BUCK

Sewanee, Tennessee
April 4, 1965

Contents

GUSTAVE FLAUBERT

by

STRATTON BUCK

Gustave Flaubert's lofty conception of the nature of art and of the sanctity of the artist's calling has made him an almost legendary figure in the history of nineteenth-century letters. Following Flaubert's career as an artist from its schoolboy beginnings until the moment when the writer collapsed over the unfinished manuscript of *Bouvard and Pecuchet,* this survey provides the reader with a thorough, up-to-date introduction to one of the world's great novelists.

Apart from discussing the works themselves, the author has undertaken to examine and analyze Flaubert's conception of beauty as it is expressed in his correspondence. He then studies the lifetime of effort which the novelist devoted to the realization of this ideal—an ideal embodied in the near perfection of *Madame Bovary* or the short story "A Simple Heart." The genesis of each of the novels is pinpointed; then evolution and development of theme, composition and elaboration are traced. The nature and content of each of the stories is described in some detail; critical evaluations of the meaning and significance of the several novels follow.

From his legend Gustave Flaubert emerges here as a man who labored always and with conscious aesthetic to bring to the novel a new dignity in the hierarchy of literary forms. The measure of his success was considerable.

Chronology

1810   Elisa Foucault (Madame Schlésinger) born at Vernon, and Louise Revoil (Madame Colet), at Aix-en-Provence.

1812   Dr. Achille-Cléophas Flaubert marries Caroline Fleuriot at Rouen.

1813   Birth of their first child, Achille Flaubert.

1816   Birth of Alfred Le Poittevin.

1819   Dr. Flaubert becomes chief surgeon at the Hotel-Dieu. The family moves into the apartment in the wing of the hospital, a perquisite of the position.
        Birth of Gertrude Collier.

1820   Birth of Ernest Chevalier.

1821   Birth of Gustave Flaubert (December 12th); birth of Louis Bouilhet.

1822   Birth of Maxime Du Camp.

1824   Birth of Caroline Flaubert (Madame Hamard), sixth and last child of the surgeon (three died in infancy).

1825   Julie, the servant of *Un Coeur simple*, enters the Flaubert household; remains there until after the death of the novelist.

1830   January 1, earliest letter in the *Correspondence* (to his grandmother). Enthusiasm for *Don Quixote*. The billiard room theater, with his sister, Alfred and Laure Le Poittevin, and Ernest Chevalier as collaborators, dates from about this time.

1832   Flaubert enters the eighth form in the Collège Royal de Rouen.

1833   Trip to Paris, Versailles, Fontainebleau, Nogent-sur-Seine.

1834   Flaubert, at school, writes tales and edits a manuscript newspaper. Summer at Trouville.

1835   Reads Shakespeare. Makes outlines of historical plays. Summer trip to Paris and Nogent-sur-Seine. Louis Bouilhet enters the *Collège*.

1836 Abundant literary production: *Deux Mains sur une couronne, Un parfum à sentir, La Peste à Florence, Rage et Impuissance,* and others. Summer at Trouville; meets Madame Schlésinger and is engulfed by a hopeless passion.

1837 Continued composition: *Rêve d'enfer, Quidquid Volueris, Passion et Vertu,* etc. Contributes "Une Leçon d'histoire naturelle: genre commis" to the *Colibri,* a Rouen paper. He and his friends invent the character *Le Garçon,* a prototype of M. Homais.

1838 *Loys XI* drame, *La Danse des Morts, Ivre et Mort,* etc. Probably began the *Mémoires d'un fou,* the earliest premonition of the *Education sentimentale.*

1839 *Smahr,* earliest sketch of *Le Tentation de Saint-Antoine, Rome et les Césars,* etc. Flaubert leaves the *Collège;* prepares for the baccalaureate examination alone. Marriage of Achille Flaubert.

1840 Obtains the baccalaureate degree. Trip with Dr. Jules Cloquet to the Pyrenees and Corsica. At Marseille, a hotel encounter leads to a brief, sultry affair with Eulalie Foucaud (not to be confused with Elisa Foucault Schlésinger). Composes travel notes: *Pyrénés, Corse.*

1841 Flaubert apparently spends the academic year 1840–41 in idleness at Rouen. Summer visits to Nogent-sur-Seine and Trouville. In the fall, registers at the Law School in Paris, but returns home determined to prepare for the first examination alone.

1842 Law study and literature. Renewal of intimacy with the Schlésingers. In September, a vacation at Trouville. Makes the acquaintance of the Collier family, who spend October in Rouen so that Dr. Flaubert may continue treating their daughter Harriet. Flirtation with Gertrude Collier. Composition of a part of the *Mémoires d'un fou?* Completion of *Novembre.* Back in Paris in November, settles in apartment on the rue de l'Est. Passes first year law examination.

1843 Paris and law school. Forms an intimate friendship with Maxime Du Camp. Begins the first version of the *Education sentimentale.* In August, Flaubert fails the second year law examination. Meets Victor Hugo in the Pradier studio. Continues to visit the Colliers and the Schlésingers.

1844   In January, the first nervous attack on the road to Pont l'Evêque. Flaubert abandons law school, and lives as a semi-invalid at home. In May, Dr. Flaubert purchases and takes possession of the estate at Croisset. Flaubert, now able to devote himself wholly to literature, continues composition of the first *Education sentimentale.*

1845   In January, the manuscript is completed. Marriage of Caroline Flaubert and Emile Hamard. The Flaubert family accompanies the newlyweds on their trip to Italy. In Genoa, in May, Flaubert sees the Breughel painting which is to inspire *La Tentation de Saint-Antoine.* Milan, Geneva, Besançon. In June, back at Croisset, he analyzes Voltaire's plays.

1846   January 15: death of Dr. Flaubert. Beginning of intimacy with Louis Bouilhet. July 30: beginning of liaison with Louise Colet, whom he had met at Pradier's studio. August 4: first letter to the Muse. September: first rendezvous with Louise Colet at the Hôtel du Grand-Cerf at Mantes.

1847   In May, Flaubert and Du Camp undertake a three-month trip, largely on foot, through the Touraine and Brittany. Each writing alternate chapters, they compose *Par les Champs et par les grèves* on their return.

1848   On February 23, Flaubert and Bouilhet rush to Paris to observe the revolution "from the point of view of art." On May 24, Flaubert begins the first version of *La Tentation de Saint-Antoine.* In June, Hamard, Flaubert's brother-in-law, shows signs of mental disturbance and threatens to demand custody of his daughter. Flaubert and his mother take the child to Forges-les-Eaux, where they make a stay of some length. Some aspects of Yonville may be suggested by Forges.

1849   Dr. Cloquet advises Flaubert to travel in warm climes. Du Camp suggests that his friend accompany him on a trip through the Near East. Flaubert continues work on *La Tentation de Saint-Antoine,* which he finishes September

12th. November 4: Flaubert, Du Camp, and a Corsican servant sail from Marseille. Alexandria, Cairo, the pyramids, Memphis.

1850 Five-month trip on a cangia up the Nile to the second cataract and return. The two friends spend a night with the courtesan, Kutchiuk-Hanem. Thebes, the Red Sea, Beyrouth, the Holy Land; Rhodes, Constantinople, Athens.

1851 Sparta, Thermopyle, the Parthenon, the Peloponnesus. Patras, Brindisi, Naples. On March 28th, the travelers arrive at Rome where they are met by Flaubert's mother. Du Camp returns to Paris, but Flaubert remains in Rome until May, and then visits Florence, Venice, Cologne, and Brussels. He is back at Croisset in June. In July, the liaison with Louise Colet is resumed. September: trip to the London Exposition; the beginning of *Madame Bovary*.

1852 Year devoted to composition of *Madame Bovary*, Part I, and Part II, Chapters 1-3; respite only for reunions, every three months, with Louise Colet, now at Paris, now at Mantes. In July, Flaubert attends the *Comices agricoles* at Grand-Couronne to prepare for the famous chapter in the novel.

1853 Composition of *Madame Bovary* continues (Part II, Chapters 4-8); likewise the meetings with Louise Colet. In the summer, a stay of four weeks at Trouville provokes a crisis of nostalgic recollection. Bouilhet leaves Rouen to settle in Paris.

1854 *Madame Bovary* (Part II, Chapters 9-13). Visits to Paris in February, May, and November. Definitive rupture with Louise Colet.

1855 *Madame Bovary* (Part II, Chapters 13-15; Part III, Chapters 1-8). March 6: from Paris, last letter to Louise Colet. September: trip to Trouville. October: with the manuscript of *Madame Bovary* all but complete, Flaubert acquires an apartment in Paris, 42, boulevard du Temple, where, henceforth, he will live several months a year.

1856 *Madame Bovary* completed. Du Camp agrees to publish it in *La Revue de Paris*. The novel, somewhat bowdlerized appears in six installments between October 1st and December 15th. Meanwhile, Flaubert has been preparing a new version of *La Tentation de Saint-Antoine*, two fragments of which are published in the *Artiste*.

1857 January: more selections from *Saint Anthony* appear in the *Artiste*. *Madame Bovary* is prosecuted as offensive to civic and religious morality. Efforts to quash the suit fail, but on February 7th, the court acquits Flaubert and the editors. Fearing further harassment, the novelist postpones the publication of *La Tentation;* his next work will be about Carthage. April: the publisher, Michel Lévy, brings out *Madame Bovary* in two volumes. The work receives widespread acclaim. In the fall, Flaubert works on the opening chapter of *Carthage,* shortly to be entitled *Salammbô*.

1858 In Paris for the winter; visits with Sainte-Beuve, Gautier, Renan, Feydeau, the Goncourt brothers, Jeanne de Tourbey, and *La Présidente*, Madame Sabatier. April 16–June 12: trip to Tunisia to study the site of Carthage. July–December: at Croisset, Flaubert rewrites Chapter 1 and prepares chapters 2 and 3 of *Salammbô*.

1859 Flaubert works on *Salammbô* (Chapters 4–7). February–June: he is resident in Paris. Louise Colet, in a keyed novel, *Lui*, publishes an unflattering portrait of her former lover.

1860 *Salammbô*, Chapters 7–10.

1861 *Salammbô*, Chapters 11–14. In June, he resolves not to leave Croisset until he has finished his book. According to the actress, Suzanne Lagier, who visits him at Croisset late this year, "labor and solitude are unhinging his mind."

1862 In January, Flaubert learns of the mental illness of Madame Schlésinger, who has been hospitalized at Baden. In February, at Paris, he finishes *Salammbô*. Lévy brings out *Salammbô* on November 24th. At the end of December, Flaubert prepares his reply to Sainte-Beuve's strictures on the novel.

1863 Great social activity. Flaubert frequents the salon of Princess Mathilda; attends the Magny dinners, where he meets Turgenev; calls upon Taine. In January, he writes the first of the precious series of letters to George Sand; also composes his answer to Froehner's attack on the historical validity of *Salammbô*. In March, back at Croisset, still uncertain as to the subject of his next novel. Reads several

Balzac novels. In August and September, at Croisset again, he collaborates with Bouilhet and d'Osmoy in the composition of a fairy play (*féerie*) which will never reach the stage. In November, he returns to Paris for the winter.

1864 Prepares outline of the *Education sentimentale*. After trips for documentation to Melun, Montereau, and Sens, he begins, in September, the composition of the new novel.

1865 Composition of the *Education sentimentale*, Part I.

1866 The *Education sentimentale*, Part II, Chapters 1 and 2. Made a *Chevalier de la Légion d honneur*. In August, and again in November, George Sand is his guest at Croisset.

1867 The *Education sentimentale*, Part II, Chapters 3–6. Resident in Paris, February through May. In March, reunion with Madame Schlésinger in Mantes or Paris or both.

1868 The *Education sentimentale*, Part III, Chapters 1–3. February through May, resident in Paris. Frequent visits with Princess Mathilda at Paris and Saint-Gratien. George Sand and Turgenev visit Croisset.

1869 Completes the *Education sentimentale* on May 16th. In June, the author begins the final revision of the *Tentation de Saint-Antoine*. Close relations with Edmond Laporte. Publication of the *Education sentimentale*, which is greeted by a generally hostile press.

1870 January through April at Paris and in poor health. At Croisset, Flaubert works on *St. Anthony*. War. In November, Prussian troops are quartered at Croisset, while Flaubert and his mother take refuge in Rouen.

1871 The war and Commune leave Flaubert depressed and bitter. Flaubert completes the fifth part of the final *St. Anthony* and settles in Paris at the end of the month.

1872 On January 17th, Flaubert writes a bitter open letter to the Municipal Council of Rouen, which has rejected the proposal of a monument to Bouilhet. In February, Bouilhet's *Dernières Chansons* are published under Lévy's imprint, with a preface by Flaubert. Quarrel and rupture between publisher and novelist. Finishes *St. Anthony*.

1873 Warm, avuncular interest in the young Guy de Maupassant, who returns the affection. Visits to the Princess at Saint-Gratien, and, with Turgenev, to George Sand at Nohant.

Contracts with the publisher, Charpentier, for *Bovary, Salammbô,* and *St. Anthony.* In September, he writes a four-act comedy, *Le Candidat.*

1874   In March, *Le Candidat* fails after four showings. In April, Charpentier publishes *Le Tentation de Saint-Antoine.* Good sale, but cool critical reception. Trips to Switzerland and Normandy for documentation for *Bouvard et Pécuchet.* Begins the composition of this work.

1875   In Paris from January to May. Composition of *Bouvard.* His health and his morale are poor, has financial problems. *Bouvard* is, for the moment, abandoned. At Concarneau, in October, he begins *La Légende de Saint-Julien l'Hospitalier.*

1876   Flaubert finishes *St. Julian;* begins and completes *Un Coeur simple;* begins *Hérodias.*

1877   At Croisset, in January, he completes *Hérodias.* After periodical publication, Charpentier brings out the *Trois Contes* in April. Critical acclaim but slow sale. In June, at Croisset, he returns to *Bouvard et Pécuchet,* and stays at work until the end of the year.

1878   Continues work on *Bouvard.* Through the fall and winter: mediocre health and financial worries. Regular work on *Bouvard.*

1879   Composition of *Bouvard et Pécuchet.* On January 25th, Flaubert slips on the ice and breaks his leg. An effort, by his friends, to have the novelist appointed librarian at the Mazarine fails. In June, the government appoints him to a sinecure which will pay 3000 francs a year. In September, he makes his last visit to Saint-Gratien and returns to Croisset, never to leave again.

1880   He begins the final chapter of *Bouvard.* On May 8th, as he is about to leave for Paris, Gustave Flaubert dies suddenly, apparently of a cerebral hemorrhage.

1881   Posthumous publication of *Bouvard et Pécuchet.* Madame Commanville sells the house at Croisset, which, except for the entrance pavillion, is razed. Maxime Du Camp publishes his *Souvenirs littéraires,* which anger Flaubert's other friends.

1884   Publication of Flaubert's letters to George Sand.

1888   Death of Elisa Schlésinger.

1890   At Rouen, dedication of a monument to Flaubert.

1909   The publisher Conard begins the *Oeuvres complètes* of Flaubert.

1921   Dedication of a bust of Flaubert, by Clésinger, in the Luxembourg Gardens at Paris.

1931   Death of Caroline Hamard Commanville Franklin-Grout. The manuscripts of the novels and other documents are left to libraries in Paris and Rouen. Many papers are sold and dispersed.

Gustave Flaubert

CHAPTER 1

By Way of Introduction

Mais il m'est resté de ce que j'ai vu—senti—et lu, une inextinguible soif de vérité, Goethe s'écriait en mourant: "De la lumière! de la lumière." Oh! oui, de la lumière, dût-elle nous brûler jusqu'aux entrailles. C'est une grande volupté que d'apprendre, que de s'assimiler le Vrai par l'intermédiaire du Beau. L'état idéal résultant de cette joie me semble une espèce de sainteté, qui est peut-être plus haute que l'autre, parce qu'elle est plus désintéressée."

To begin with the legend, Gustave Flaubert lives for us as the incarnation of the Artist. His life constituted one long act of devotion to literature. From childhood forward, his only ambition was to be a writer. A small income freed him from mundane cares; he was able, therefore, to devote his every energy to his lofty conception of his calling. At the age of twenty-two, he cut himself off from the main current of the life of his day and retired to his estate at Croisset, near Rouen, to live henceforth as a near hermit. He never married. Convinced that action and contemplative creation were incompatible, he systematically refused himself the distractions and satisfactions of normal involvement in the life of this world. His exclusive devotion to Art kept him, day after day and year after year, in the study at Croisset, projecting plans, accumulating and sifting data, writing, striking out, writing, discarding, and writing again. He was never content to abandon a sentence until he was sure that he had achieved the most adequate expression of which he was capable.

He wrote to please himself, with no thought for wealth or fame. His standards were exacting; his labors, prodigious. Over a period of thirty years, he produced only six books, averaging nearly five years for the composition of a novel. But the work went on. One after the other, *Madame Bovary, Salammbô,* the *Education sentimentale,* the *Tentation de Saint-Antoine,* and the *Trois Contes* took shape, were polished, and emerged from the study table to the light of day. He died at the age of fifty-eight, tired to the bones, but still laboring on the manuscript of his posthumous work, *Bouvard et Pécuchet.* Posterity has consecrated his greatness.

This legend, illuminating and meaningful, is, in its broad lines, essentially true. There was, of course, a non-legendary person named Gustave Flaubert who lived the life of flesh and blood in the France of the mid-nineteenth century. The hermit did escape from Croisset. He traveled widely—in France, in England, over the whole Mediterranean coast, and through much of the Near East. He knew the friendship of men and the love of women. During the winter months, he occupied an apartment in Paris, where he entertained regularly and led an active social life. He was not wholly insensitive to glory and fame. He was pleased to be invited to the Emperor's receptions at the Tuileries, and he was flattered to be part of the intimate coterie of Princess Mathilda. Due in part to his own generosity, he was ruined, late in life, by the bankruptcy of his niece and her husband. The financial distress of his last years was compensated for, in part, by the devotion of a group of admiring friends. He was not, therefore, the disembodied spirit that the myth sometimes suggests. But the important center of the picture is nonetheless the study at Croisset, and Flaubert's lifelong dedication to Truth apprehended through Beauty is more than a pious legend.

CHAPTER 2

The Correspondence: Ideas and Temperament

1.

"je voulais faire une colonne toute nue."

IN addition to the six books already mentioned, Flaubert left a masterpiece in the thirteen volumes of his personal letters. There are readers who consider his greatest work to be his correspondence. In any case, it gives us precious insights into the temperament and opinions of this novelist who sought to hide his life and whose esthetic principles led him to attempt to keep himself and his personality out of his published writing. The earliest letters date from his ninth year; the last was penned a few days before his sudden death in 1880.

This correspondence makes it possible for us to follow almost from day to day Flaubert's intimate life and thought. It reveals, as nothing else can, his many-sided, frequently contradictory personality: his mystic devotion to Beauty and Art, and his immense disgust with human existence; his life of incredible sacrifice and labor, and his conviction that nothing is worth the effort; his warmth and generosity, his bitterness and his cynicism. These magnificent enthusiasms, splendid anathemas, striking generalizations on life and art and history, all expressed with a passion and a wealth of imagination and metaphor, contrast strikingly with the careful polish of the style of the novels. The letters discuss in detail the composition of the stories and the problems that beset the author in his efforts to fulfill his intentions. Flaubert never wrote the three prefaces, in which he planned to give systematic expression to his esthetic beliefs. The letters do not, of course, constitute such an expression; but from them we can gather the ideas of which this statement would have been composed. Flaubert never made good his intention of writing his own memoirs, but many of the features that would have gone into the autobiographical portrait can be inferred from the letters. The intention of this chapter is both to introduce the reader to portions of this too little-known correspondence and to derive from them a notion of the temperament and artistic ideas of the author.

Born in 1821, Flaubert became of age as the great flood waters of Romanticism were beginning to ebb. Goethe, Byron, Chateaubriand, and Hugo were among his earliest literary enthusiasms. His juvenile writings, more successful than those of many authors and important for students of his biography, are lyrical confessions of longing and despair. To the end of his life, he choked with affection and regret whenever he evoked the dear dead days and the youth that he had been.

How was your youth spent? Mine was inwardly very beautiful. I had enthusiasms which, alas, I no longer find. Friends who are dead or metamorphized. A great confidence in myself, superb leaps of the soul, something impetuous in all my person. I dreamed of love, of glory, of the Beautiful. My heart was as broad as the world and I breathed in all the winds of heaven. And then, bit by bit, I became shriveled, worn, faded. Oh! I accuse no one but myself. I submerged myself in senseless sentimental gymnastics. I took pleasure in combatting my senses and torturing my heart. I repulsed the human intoxications which were offered. Bent on struggling against myself, I uprooted the man with two hands, two hands full of force and pride. Out of that tree with verdant foliage I wanted to make a bare column, in order to place, at the very top, as on an altar, I know not what celestial flame. That is why, I find myself, at the age of thirty-six, so empty and sometimes so tired. Is not this story of mine that I tell you a little bit your own? [1]

The explanation of this process of self-mutilation, as the closing question to his correspondent implies, is to be found in part in the date at which he became aware of himself and his aspirations. As indicated earlier, the Romantic movement had run its course. The generation of Flaubert, which became of age in the 1840's, nourished though it had been by the great lyric creation of its predecessors, was forced to take stock, to judge, to react, and to seek new ways. Further plumbing in the veins exploited by the masters of 1830 could only produce secondhand and anachronistic works. And the excesses of Romanticism were too obvious, its falsities too evident. So a generation characterized by an exuberance of creative genius unparalleled perhaps in the history of literature gave way to a posterity which was to value critical intelligence, erudition, and technical perfection. The foliage and limbs of the luxuriant tree were pruned away to provide the bare column with the celestial fire at its top. Flaubert's story is not unlike that of his peers and contemporaries: Taine, Renan, Leconte de Lisle, and Baudelaire. Flaubert is the child of his generation.

This generation, taken as a group, was pessimistic about the condition and destiny of man. It could not believe, as had Hugo and Balzac, in the redeeming power of passion, energy, and will—in the ability of human genius to cope with the problems of this world. It had seen the Romantic effort to scale the heavens and to force the sanctuary collapse in defeat. It had seen the utopian aspirations of 1848 lead to brutal reaction and to the military government of Napoleon III. It was imbued with a mechanistic conception of the physical and biological sciences that appeared to deny spiritual or human values. There could be no salvation in this world or the next.

For Gustive Flaubert, this pessimism led very early to disgust and horror for life in this world:

What is it that made me so old as I left my cradle, and so disgusted by happiness before I had even drunk of it? All that has to do with life is repugnant to me; everything that draws me to it and plunges me in it horrifies me. I should like never to have been born, or to die. I have within me, deep within me, a distaste which keeps me from enjoying anything and which fills my soul to the point of suffocating it. It reappears in relation to everything, like the bloated bodies of dogs which come back to the surface of the water despite the stones that have been tied to their necks to drown them. (I, 429)

This paragraph, which is characteristic, reveals something more personal, more fundamental, than a philosophic judgment on the human condition. It is a visceral repugnance, a cringing of the very flesh before the facts of existence. The intellectual temper of the age, while it confirmed and strengthened his bitterness, could hardly have caused it.

Biographers have sought its source in the circumstances of his life, and Flaubert did indeed endure his share of vicissitude, disappointment, and tragedy. But his pessimism antedated both the onset of his nervous illness and his experience of woes of life in this world. As he said, he was old and disgusted from the moment he left his cradle:

I have deep in my soul the fog of the North that I breathed at my birth. I carry within me the melancholy of the barbarian races, with their instinct for migrations and their innate disgust for life which made them flee their land as if to flee themselves. They loved the sun, all those barbarians who went to die in Italy; they had a frenetic aspiration toward light, toward the blue sky, toward some warm and sonorous existence; they dreamed of happy days, full of loves as juicy for their hearts as the ripe grape that one presses with his hands. I have always had for them a tender sympathy, as for ancestors. Did I not find in their noisy story my whole, peaceful, unknown tale? Alaric's cries of joy as he entered Rome had for parallel, fourteen centuries later, the secret deliriums of a poor child's heart. (I, 217)

For Flaubert, then, his tedium was innate. It was the inheritance of the land in which he was born and the race from which he had sprung. Perhaps. But these sentences also reveal eloquently what we call a Romantic longing for fairer suns and bluer skies and more exotic climes. It is *le mal du siècle* uniquely intense and persistent, perhaps, in Flaubert. It is the product of an acute, powerful imagination which makes the concept precede the experience—the image of the sensation precede the sensation itself. And the concept and the image are too rare for the realities of this world. The experience is a mean thing compared to the dream of the experience. It is the story of Madame Bovary for whom the reality of love would not conform to her preconception and more exotic climes. It is *le mal du siècle* uniquely intense and the explanation of his bitterness and disillusionment. He had lived a warmer and more sonorous life:

It seems to me that I have always existed and that I possess memories that date back to the Pharaohs. I see myself at different ages in history, distinctly, practicing different trades and in multiple states of fortune. My present individuality is the product of my vanished individualities. I have been a boatman on the Nile, a pander at Rome at the time of the Punic wars, then a Greek rhetor at Suburra where I was devoured by bedbugs. I died during the Crusades because of having eaten too many grapes on the beach of Syria. I have been a pirate and a monk, a mountebank and a coach driver. Perhaps Emperor of the Orient, too.

Many things would be explained if we could know our real genealogy. For the elements that make a man being limited, the same combinations must be reproduced. So heredity is a sound principle which has been poorly applied. (V, 240)

Flaubert's *Vie antérieure* (or perhaps we should say his *Vies antérieures*) was rich, varied, and specific. It is customary to speak of the *mal du siècle,* as I have just done—or of the hypertrophy of Romantic imagination. We are also before one of the by-products of a sophisticated age. His historical imagination had been fed by omnivorous, precocious reading. He possessed, to a very high degree, the power to give his ideas specific, plastic form. He could see himself clearly and distinctly as a pirate, or a crusader, or a rhetor, performing well-conceived deeds against a perfectly visualized background. This power of imagination was an advantage for the artist, but its very wealth contributed not a little to the disillusionment and bitterness of the man.

As the conclusion of the excerpt suggests, Flaubert's real genealogy is to be found far more surely in his imaginary incarnations, in his vicarious experience, than in any fancied influence of northern mists, or supposed inheritance from barbarian migrants. In the splendor of his inner life, as an adolescent and young man, he had lived the whole panorama of history, its color and its strangeness, its drama and its meaning. Small wonder that he could not adapt himself to the dull, petty insignificance of contemporary life.

Time and disappointment, as we shall see, were to teach Flaubert to criticize and control his imaginative flights. His work takes the form of a long commentary on the tragic disparity between the splendor of the dream and the meanness of the reality— between the magnificence of the concept and the tawdriness of the thing. This is the mutilation mentioned at the start of this discussion. But Flaubert never renounced or condemned the exuberance of his youth.

It seems to me that there are things that I alone feel and that others have not said and that I can say. This sorrowful side of modern man, that you notice, is the fruit of my youth. I spent a good one with my poor Alfred [le Poittevin]. We lived in an ideal hothouse in which poetry heated our *"embêtement"* with existence to seventy Réaumur degrees. He was a man. Never have I made such trips across space. We went far, without leaving our hearth. We flew high, although the ceiling of my room was low. There are afternoons that have remained in my head, conversations of six consecutive hours, walks along our hillsides and tedium shared, tedium, tedium. All memories which appear to me colored in vermilion, and flame behind me like a conflagration. (II, 362 f.)

Between the world and me existed I know not what stained glass, painted yellow with streaks of fire and arabesques of gold, so that everything was reflected on my soul as on the tiles of a sanctuary, embellished, transfigured and yet melancholy—and nothing walked there that was not beautiful. There were dreams more majestic and more vested than cardinals in purple copes. . . . When I am old, to write all that will warm me up again. I shall do like those who, before leaving for a long trip, go bid adieu to beloved tombs. I, before I die, shall visit my dreams again.

Well, it is very fortunate to have had such a youth and no one to thank you for it. Oh, if I had been loved at the age of 17, what an idiot I would be today. (III, 130)

The tree's limbs were pruned away; but, without the first luxuriant foliage, there could have been no lofty trunk on which to display the celestial flame. The romantic dreams of Flaubert's youth were the precondition of the novelist's genius. One is fortunate to have had such a youth.

It is important, however, not to attempt to realize the dream in the world of life and action. This, I take it, is the meaning of the closing sentence of the passage. If the author had been loved at the age of seventeen, before this critical sense had developed, the effort to live the ideal, and its inevitable collapse, would have led to a compromise with the conditions of life in this world, and "what an idiot I would be today." It is the acceptance of the tawdry circumstances of life, the failure to recognize the disparity between the dream and the possible, that makes fools and liars of men. If one is to be true to himself and to his dream, he must first of all accept the fact that happiness is not possible in this world: "How badly arranged the world is. What is the purpose of ugliness, suffering, sadness? Why our powerless dreams? Why everything? I lived for several years in a state of mind that I dare to qualify as epic without feeling the slightest doubt or the slightest fatigue. But at present, I am broken." (IV, 159)

Such complaints recur, in the correspondence, again and again. Our dreams are powerless. The world is composed of ugliness, suffering, and sadness. The purpose of it all, if there be one, escapes us. The very word "happiness" is a snare: "Have you reflected at times, dear and tender old friend, on how many tears that horrible word 'happiness' has caused to flow? Without that word, one would sleep more peacefully and live more at ease. I am taken now and again by strange aspirations toward love, although I am disgusted with it to the very marrow. They would perhaps pass unnoticed if I were not always attentive and sharp-eyed in observing my heart." (I, 185)

This awareness of the disparity between the dream and the reality, and this loathing for the pettiness and senselessness of life inform Flaubert's entire work. A discussion of them is essential to an understanding of the man and of the author.

2.

"je ne sais quelle flamme céleste"

The bare column represents a mutilation. It symbolizes an act of will; a determination on the part of Flaubert to root out and to destroy what seemed to be his inner self; to renounce the lyricism of his dreams of love and glory; "to combat his senses and torture his heart." It is possible to regret that this act was performed. It is possible to believe that Flaubert's conclusions on the meanness of existence and the absence of human values in the universe are mistaken and unfortunate. It is possible to wish that the foliage had not been pruned away. But the justification for the sentimental gymnastics is clear. The bare column was to serve as an altar for "I know not what celestial flame." This celestial flame, of course, is his mystic conception of Beauty, Art, and the Artist's calling:

My life, at least, has never faltered. From the time when I wrote asking my nurse for the letters it was necessary to use to form the words of the sentences I was inventing until this evening when the ink is drying on the crossed out words of my pages, I have followed a straight line, unceasingly prolonged and drawn like a cord across everything. I have always seen the goal draw back before me, from year to year, from progress to progress. How many times I have fallen flat on my belly just at the moment when I seemed to be touching it. I feel none the less that I am not to die without having made roar, somewhere, a style like the one I hear in my head and which will be quite able to dominate the voices of the parrots and cicadas. (II, 440)

Flaubert, indeed, received the call of letters as a child, and he never faltered in his determination to become an artist. It would perhaps be more accurate to say that he never conceived of himself in any other role: "It happened that my organization is a system; all without conscious purpose, by the propensity of things which makes the white bear inhabit the ice and the camel walk on the sand. I am a man whose hand holds a pen. I feel through it, because of it, in relationship to it, and much more with it." (II, 364) He existed, primarily in his function as a writer; his personal life was subordinate to this function. And the practice of Art, as Flaubert understood it, was exacting beyond measure: "I have finished, since you saw me, 25 clean pages (25 pages in six weeks). They were hard to push. I have worked on them, recopied them, changed them, recast them, to such an extent that for the moment I see only fire." (II, 394)

Composition was laborious. The polished sentences, the perfect phraseology, the harmonies and striking cadences that mark Flaubert's prose, did not come easily. Six weeks of effort to produce twenty-five pages—five years on the average to complete a volume—the work was slow, demanding, frustrating:

I lead a bitter life, devoid of all external joy and in which I have nothing to keep me going but a sort of permanent rage, which weeps at times from impotence, but which is constant. I love my work with a frenetic and perverse love, as an ascetic loves the hair shirt which scratches his belly. Sometimes, when I find myself empty, when the expression refuses to come, when after scribbling long pages I discover that I have not made a sentence, I fall on my couch and lie there dazed in an interior bog of depression.

I hate myself and accuse myself for this madness which makes me pant after a chimera. A quarter of an hour later, everything is changed; my heart beats with joy. . . . I have glimpsed sometimes (in my great days of sunlight), by the glow of an enthusiasm which made my skin tingle from my heels to the roots of my hair, a state of soul far superior to life, before which glory would be nothing and happiness itself useless. . . .

Between the crowd and us, no bond. So much the worse for the crowd, so much the worse for us above all. But as everything has its reason for being, and as the fantasy of an individual seems to me quite as legitimate as the appetite of a million men, and as it can occupy as much space in the world, it is necessary, disregarding things and independently of the humanity that repudiates us, to live for our calling, to climb into our ivory tower, and there, like an Indian dancer amidst her perfumes, remain alone in our dreams. I sometimes feel great ennui, profound emptiness, doubts which sneer in my face in the midst of my most spontaneous satisfactions. Well, I would not exchange all that for anything, because it seems to me, in my conscience, that I am doing my duty, that I am obeying a superior fatality, that I am following the Good and that I am in the Right. (II, 395 f.)

This amazing letter was written to Louise Colet in April, 1852, early in the period of the composition of *Madame Bovary*. Similar passages abound through the *Correspondence*, but this one provides the most complete expression of the faith which inspired both the man and his work. Flaubert's Art is his god. Beauty exists. The language of his devotion is that of the Christian ascetic, to whom he compares himself. Despite the meanness and stupidity of the world, despite the dreariness of the task and the narrowness of the path, despite the doubts that sneer in his face, Flaubert, like Saint Anthony, kneels in prayer, convinced that he is doing his duty, that what he is doing is good, and that he is in the right. This mystique explains his work and justifies his life.

As critics have pointed out, there is an ambiguity here. It is difficult to see how Beauty and Truth can exist in a universe without values; how the Artist can give significance to the objects of a world in which everything is meaningless, and still be true to the reality. Flaubert called himself "a mystic who believes in nothing"; Paul Bourget labelled him a nihilist athirst for the absolute. But faith there is.

Anthony Thorlby[2] goes much too far, in my opinion, when he says that Flaubert claimed no higher value for the object of his devotion. It is true that the letters offer countless examples of the doubts that, throughout his life, sneered in his face. It is likewise true that the metaphysical difficulty is real and that Flaubert was conscious of it. The *Correspondence* can hardly be expected to provide a full and systematic philosophy. But the discussions of esthetics in the letters are predominantly statements of faith; and, as René de Week has put it, Flaubert's life was one long spiritual exercise.[3] His asceticism, his struggle to cast out the old man and to win his salvation, despite the temptations of his passions and the world, bear witness to his faith in the higher value of his Art.

3.

"L'auteur, dans son oeuvre doit être comme Dieu dans son univers, présent partout, et visible nulle part."

Flaubert never liked the word "realism." Not only did he distrust labels and schools, but he felt that his contemporaries and friends who had rallied to this concept had lost sight of the real nature of literary art—or were, at least, emphasizing the wrong things. His reply to George Sand is characteristic:

Speaking of my friends, you add "my school." But I ruin my temperament by trying not to have a school. *A priori*, I reject them all. Those whom I see often and whom you indicate strive for all that I scorn and have mediocre concern for what torments me. I consider the technical detail, the bit of local information, the whole historical and exact side of things as very secondary. I strive above all for *beauty*, which my companions seek only to a mediocre degree.   (VII, 281)

It is difficult to take the negative side of such disclaimers seriously. From the beginning to the end of his career, and in every one of his six volumes, Flaubert gave what many people believe is inordinate attention to historical and geographical accuracy, to the technical detail that he claimed to consider secondary. This criticism of Hugo's *Les Misérables* is closer to his practice: "Observation is a secondary quality in literature, but it is not per-

missible to paint society so falsely when one is the contem
of Balzac and Dickens." (V, 36)

Flaubert was likewise the contemporary and the friend of
and Renan, and he accepted the determinism and the assum
of his Realistic generation. The method of the scientist, the
tion of the historian, the pursuit, to use Taine's phrase, of *le*
fait vrai, indisputable, significatif informed and inspired
bert's thinking and his work:

History, history and natural history. These are the two mu:
the modern age. With them, we shall enter new, new worlds.
Let us observe, that is everything. And after centuries of st
perhaps someone will be permitted to make the synthesis. . .
greatest geniuses, the greatest works have never concluded. H
Shakespeare, Goethe, all the eldest sons of God (as Michelet s
have taken good care to do nothing but represent. (V, 111)

Observation must, therefore, precede representation. The a
must be a "triple thinker." He must see better and farther
other men; he must apprehend the object in its uniqueness an
its universal significance.

For Flaubert, this demand involved contemplation, study,
research. The amount of erudition that went into *Salammbô,*
Education sentimentale, the *Tentation de Saint-Antoine*, or
Madame Bovary would do honor to a German dissertation. I
ing the preparation of each novel, the author absorbed and
notes from countless volumes, brochures, and newspaper
counts. He harried his friends for hard to get information—a
stock market operations in 1847 or railroad schedules in 1848.
Salammbô, he studied, among countless other subjects, the ph
cal symptoms of starvation in human beings and the disease
serpents. In the line of duty, he witnessed operations, atten
county fairs, and observed the manufacture of porcelain. He
unable to proceed with the composition of *Salammbô* until he
visited the site of Carthage. He made the trips and did the erra
that his protagonists were to make or do in Rouen, Paris, Nog
Fontainebleau, Pont l'Evêque, and elsewhere. While writing
Coeur simple, he kept a stuffed parrot on his study table. H
ever secondary he may have considered such details, his d

mentation was elaborate, laborious, scrupulous. The representation was to be based on observation so close and so accurate as to make us "feel almost materially, the things he is describing."

Exactitude of detail is essential if the whole is to be true to life. And truth is morality: "I try naïvely to be as comprehensive as possible. What more can one ask of me. . . . If the reader does not derive from a book the morality that ought to be there, it is because the reader is an imbecile or because the book is false from the point of view of exactitude. From the moment that a thing is true, it is good. Obscene books even are immoral only because they lack truth. Things don't happen 'that way' in life." (VII, 285)

To be comprehensive, however, does not mean to be inclusive. Selection, for Flaubert, implies choosing the detail that will reveal the object in its characteristic and universal significance. Criticizing an incident in a novel by René de Mauricourt, Flaubert wrote: "I ask you frankly whether that is ordinary in life? Now the novel, which is its scientific form, must proceed by generalities and be more logical than the hazard of things." (V, 179) The accidents, the sports, the exceptions are not the subject matter of art: "I have always forced myself to go to the soul of things and to limit myself to the broadest generalities, and I have turned away intentionally from the accidental and the dramatic. No heroes and no monsters." (VII, 281) To apprehend life in its scientific form, to reach the soul of things, and to perceive the broadest generalities, the artist must look outside himself. Neither passion nor prejudice can be permitted to deform or falsify his observation of reality.

Flaubert's doctrine of impersonaltiy is based on esthetic, philosophical, and personal considerations. He was persuaded that the greatest writers, "the elder sons of God," had represented the world objectively and had kept their feelings out of their work:

You will come to pity the practice of singing about yourself. It succeeds sometimes in a cry, but whatever lyricism Byron may attain, for example, how Shakespeare crushes him in comparison with his superhuman impersonality. Do we know even whether he was sad or gay? The artist must so arrange things as to make posterity believe that he did not live. The less I can form an idea of him, the greater he seems to me. I cannot imagine anything about the passions of Homer or Rabelais, and when I think of Michaelangelo, I see, but only from

the back, an old man of colossal stature, carving, at night, by torch light. (II, 380)

The impersonality of the artist has probably never been extolled in language so intimately personal, but this is a private letter, not writing for publication. On this experience of the past, on this observation of the practice of the artists he admires above all others, Flaubert constructs a dogma:

> It is one of my principles that one must not write about himself. The artist in his work must be like God in creation, invisible and all powerful; let his presence be felt everywhere, but let him not be seen.
> And then, Art must rise above personal affection and nervous susceptibility. It is time to give it, by means of a pitiless method, the precision of the physical sciences. (IV, 164)

His esthetic convictions were reinforced by his preoccupation with the scientific method, and he is attracted by analogies between the physical sciences and the arts:

> To conclude, most of the time, seems to me an act of stupidity. That is what is beautiful about the natural sciences: they wish to prove nothing. Consequently, what breadth of fact and what immensity for thought. We must treat men like mastodons or crocodiles. Do we fly into a passion about the horn of the former or the jawbone of the latter? Display them, stuff them, preserve them in bottles, that's all; but *evaluate* them, no. And who do you think you are, my little toads? (III, 154)

There is also a more personal consideration, which might be described as a fear of his own neurotic nature: a lack of confidence in his ability to see things whole and clearly should he allow himself and his thought to become involved in the passions of ordinary life:

> When one wishes to concern one's self with the works of God, one must begin, simply as a matter of hygiene, by putting one's self in a position not to be their dupe. You will paint wine, love, women, glory, on the condition, my little man, that you are neither a drunkard, a lover, a husband, or a soldier. Caught up in life, you see it badly.

You suffer from it or enjoy it too much. The artist, in my opinion, is a monstrosity, something outside of nature. (II, 268)

This response was elicited by his mother's question as to whether he had any intention of taking a wife. Like the priest, the artist does not marry.

The sentences quoted above were written by a man who was not yet thirty and had never published a line. Twenty-five years later, Flaubert, then the author of several acknowledged masterpieces was, when admonished by George Sand, to justify his impersonality less pretentiously and more modestly in terms of the subordination of the man before the work:

As for my "lack of conviction," alas, convictions stifle me. I am bursting with anger and with pent-up indignation. But in the ideal that I have of Art, I believe that one should not reveal these, and that the artist should no more appear in his work than God in nature. The man is nothing, the work every-thing. This discipline, which may start from a false point of view, is not easy to observe. And for me, at least, it is a sort of permanent sacrifice that I make to good taste. It would be very agreeable to say what I think and to relieve M. Gustave Flaubert with phrases; but what is the importance of the aforementioned gentleman? (VII, 280)

The artist will not, therefore, express his opinion directly. He will not reveal his judgment of the behavior or of the attitudes of his characters. He will content himself, like the scientist, with the analysis of the essential facts and with the representation of the action and the circumstances. Any conclusions must be drawn by the reader. Great art is objective and impersonal.

Nonetheless, it seems to me that there has been a good deal of confusion about the words "Flaubert's impersonality." The artist, as we have seen, refused to let himself become *engagé* in the Sartrian sense; but the *Correspondence,* as Thibaudet reminded us years ago, was written by a man who is constantly concluding, and who expresses strong and violent personal opinions in every sentence: "Alas, convictions stifle me." If the novelist "does not have the right" to reveal these convictions in his work, the man, Flaubert, does not live in a state of eternally suspended judgment: "It is true that many things exasperate me. The day when I am no longer indignant, I shall fall flat, like a doll from which one has removed the supporting stick." (V, 309)

This indignation, this mighty anger which sustains the man, is not the Olympian aloofness, the contemptuous rejection of all involvement in life that some commentators seem to think. Nor were Flaubert's life and art the inhuman refusal of all emotion that is sometimes suggested. The personal, as we have seen, is, to the extent that it may falsify or distort the artist's vision, forbidden: "The less one feels a thing, the more qualified one is to express it as it is (as it is always in itself, in its generality, and free of all its ephemeral contingencies). But one must have the faculty for making oneself feel it." (II, 462)

This power of the imagination is possible only if it is rooted in sympathy and compassion. It is easy to talk about oneself; not so easy to reproduce the feelings of others:

The poet is required today to have sympathy for all and for everyone, in order to understand and describe them.   (IV, 243)

. . . . .

There was a time when you considered me a jealous egoist who took pleasure in the perpetual rumination of his own personality. . . . No one more than I, on the contrary, has assimilated others. I have gone to breathe the odor of unknown dung heaps, I have had compassion for many things which do not draw tears from sensitive people. If Bovary is worth anything, the book will not lack heart.   (II, 407)

Flaubert's novels are not lacking in heart. The work of art is to be presented objectively and impersonally, but it is informed nonetheless by that compassion and sympathy which alone make possible the discovery of the common bond of humanity which unites Emma, Matho, Frederic, and the others with the erudite artist in the study at Croisset.

4.

"Plus une idée est belle, plus la phrase est sonore, soyez-en sûr."

"There are neither noble nor ignoble subjects, and one could almost establish as an axiom that there are none, if one starts from the point of view of pure Art, style being in itself an absolute way

of seeing things." (II, 346) Despite the lengths to which Flaubert
went to obtain physical and psychological accuracy, his great preoccupation was elsewhere. Observation and the accumulation of
indisputably reliable data were at best only a first step; the real
function of the artist was to transmute this material into Beauty
by the magic—Flaubert liked to say "the chemistry"—of literary
style. The idea, in its precision and in its entirety, is realized only
in the perfection of the form through which it is expressed: "You
tell me that I pay too much attention to form. Alas, it is like body
and soul, form and idea; for me it's all one, and I don't know what
one is without the other. The more beautiful an idea is, the more
sonorous is the sentence, be sure of it. Precision of thought makes
and is that of words." (IV, 243) This and countless similar pronouncements have led some commentators to conceive Flaubert's
esthetic ideal as a formal, but essentially lifeless and inhuman
perfection. The Platonic overtones of some of the striking statements have suggested to some an abstract and frozen conception
of Art, which, I believe, was far removed from Flaubert's thought
or practice; for he stated: "Literature is not an abstract thing. It
addresses itself to the whole man." (*Notes de Voyage*, II, 358)

Jean-Pierre Richard, in a recent essay, perhaps the finest written
on the novelist since the work of Albert Thibaudet, has made a
brilliant study of the creation of form by Flaubert. I am deeply
indebted to this work for much of the development which follows.

Style must, of course, impose its order on the unformed, cha-
otic substance that it molds. It must not, however, freeze the
fluidity that it contains; it must let us sense the palpitation of life
vibrating immediately under the polish. An analogy with sculp-
ture is, perhaps, helpful. Visiting Athens in 1851, Flaubert wrote
the following description of a bas relief at the Acropolis:

One of the breasts is veiled; the other bare. What a breast, my God,
what a breast. It is apple-round, full, abundant, detached from the
other, and heavy in the hand. There are in it fruitful maternities and
sweetnesses of love to make one swoon. Rain and sun have made this
white marble yellow blond. It has a tawny tone which makes it almost resemble flesh. It is so tranquil and so noble. One would say
that it is going to heave and that the lungs underneath are going to
fill and breathe. . . . How one would have rolled on it in tears. . . .
A trifle more and I should have prayed. (II, 299)

[36]

The polish of the surface, the perfection of line and curve must, therefore, not conceal the pulsation of life and soul, the possibilities and immanences underneath. Form lifts phenomena to their absolute or ideal expression, but "the ideal is fruitful only if one makes it contain everything. It is a labor of love and not of exclusion." (IV, 15) The form must *contain*, yet it must also make us aware of the virtualities of the chaos immediately underneath.

The ideas expounded by Leconte de Lisle in the Preface to the *Poèmes antiques* are not adequate to Flaubert: "There is something more to Art than rectitude of line and polish of surface. . . . It is necessary to make tableaux, to show nature as she is, but complete tableaux, to paint what is underneath and what is on the surface." (III, 157) For the literary artist, style and composition replace surface, line, and curve. But the problem is essentially the same. "Be good," Flaubert wrote Louise Colet, "work, make me some great, beautiful thing, sober and severe, something which is warm underneath and splendid on the surface." (I, 311) The splendor of the surface must be permeable to the warmth of life underneath. "It is necessary, before everything else, to have blood in one's sentences and not lymph, and when I say blood, I mean heart. It must beat, it must palpitate, it must stir response. It is necessary to make trees love and granite throb. One can put an immense love in the story of a blade of grass." (IV, 62) To paraphrase Mr. Richard, the sentence becomes a skin beneath which one feels the circulation of blood and the tremor of flesh.

Perfection is not of this world. Human speech is a defective instrument on which we are condemned "to beat out tunes for dancing bears when we would like to draw tears from the stars." "The plastic of style is not so broad as the whole idea, I know it perfectly well. But whose fault is that? The fault of language. We have too many things and not enough forms. Hence the torture of the conscientious." (III, 157) A lifetime of labor with *les affres du style* is the lot, therefore, of the sincere artist who undertakes to express himself through this untractable medium. But the frustrating search for the exact word, the struggle to eliminate assonances and repetition, the preoccupation with rhythm and sound—all the scruples which Flaubert brought to his table as he wrote, revised, and discarded—now can be seen in the perspective of the vision he glimpsed. And sometimes, in the lonely study, there were intimations of immortality: "The burdened soul unbends in this azure which stops only at the frontiers of the True. Indeed, where form is lacking, the idea no longer exists. To seek one is to seek the other. They are as inseparable as substance and color and that is why Art is Truth itself." (II, 415)

Critics have expressed incomprehension or amusement over Flaubert's desire to write a book about nothing, which would stand of its own "by the inner force of its style, as the earth, without being supported, maintains itself in the air." (II, 345) Is not Flaubert saying merely that the beauty and interest of the work of art derives, not from the subject matter, but from the style created by the constructive intelligence of the artist? "One can put an immense love in the story of a blade of grass."

The book about nothing figures in a letter written in 1852. Twenty-four years later, Flaubert reverted to the idea in an exchange with George Sand:

I do not share Turgenev's severity with respect to *Jack,* nor the immensity of his admiration for *Rougon.* One has charm and the other strength. But neither one is preoccupied, *before everything else,* with what makes for me the goal of Art, namely Beauty. I remember having had palpitations of the heart, having felt a violent pleasure contemplating a wall of the Acropolis, an entirely bare wall. . . . Well, I wonder whether a book, independently of what it says, cannot produce the same effect. In the precision of the assembly, the rarity of the elements, the polish of the surface, the harmony of the whole, is there not an intrinsic virtue, a sort of divine force, something eternal as a principle? (I speak like a platonist.) Thus why is there a necessary relationship between the exact word and the musical word? Why does it always happen that one writes a verse when one compresses his thought too much? The law of numbers then governs sentiments and images, and what seems to be the exterior is really the inside. If I continued long in this way, I would put my foot completely in my mouth, for, on the other hand, Art has got to be human.   (VII, 293)

This is the mysticism of the Flaubert esthetic, a mysticism which, as we see, did not fully satisfy him, because he could not make it include every aspect of the creative process. But despite the doubts raised by his sophisticated and skeptical critical intelligence, this was the belief that sustained him: "The concern for exterior beauty with which you reproach me is for me a method.

When I discover an unpleasant assonance or a repetition in my sentences, I am sure that I am floundering in the false. By dint of searching, I find the exact expression, which was the only one, and which is, at the same time, the harmonious one. The word is never lacking, when one is in possession of the idea." (VII, 290) In this faith, Flaubert labored.

5.

"je suis un homme-plume"

And, as M. Richard has pointed out so brilliantly, there is more at issue to Flaubert than the construction of a literary monument. The slow and laborious discovery and creation of adequate forms is, in a sense, for Flaubert, the discovery and creation of his own being. Throughout his life the novelist was faced by the anguished problem of recognizing or realizing his own identity. He could not or would not choose among the amorphous and unrealized possibilities that he felt intuitively to be present in his life: "An entire creation, unrevealed to itself, lived secretly under my life; I was a sleeping chaos of a thousand fruitful principles which did not know how to manifest themselves, nor what to do with themselves; they sought their form and awaited their mold." (*Oeuvres de Jeunesse,* II, 180)

These words, written when Flaubert was twenty, reflect a condition that was to haunt him throughout his life. The potential creation, these principles of fecundity awaited only the revelation of themselves, the form that would bring to fruition their unrealized possibilities. And in the words of M. Richard: "It is *art* alone that will be able to give it to them. Artistic creation then is, for Flaubert, tantamount to the creation of self by self: each sentence, each successful paragraph, brings him a bit further out of the slough, raises him to the solid existence the promise of which his immediate life contained in itself, but which it was reserved to his labor alone to be able finally to accomplish." [4]

Please see Note 5.

CHAPTER 3

Life, Love, Vocation

1.

"O dortoirs de mon collège, vous aviez des mélancolies plus vastes que celles que j'ai trouvées au désert."

FLAUBERT, born at Rouen in 1821, was the son of a prosperous physician who was chief-of-staff at the Hotel-Dieu; his mother, the daughter of a doctor, was descended from the Norman gentry. His brother Achille, to whom he was never close and who succeeded their father as surgeon-in-chief at the Hotel-Dieu, was nine years his senior. His sister, Caroline, was three years younger than he. The family ties were close and intimate—Flaubert grew up in an atmosphere marked by affection and security. The family was cultivated and literate, but his background in no way explains his precocious, exclusive devotion to Art and Beauty.

This taste was revealed early. When he was not more than nine years old, he was fascinated by *Don Quixote,* read aloud to him by a neighbor, le Père Mignot. At about the same time—in collaboration with his sister Caroline and their friends Ernest Chevalier and Alfred and Laure Le Poittevin (Laure was to become Madame de Maupassant, and the mother of the short-story writer)—he wrote tragedies and comedies which the group produced before relatives and servants at the Flaubert apartment in the Hotel-Dieu, Dr. Flaubert's billiard table serving as the stage.

The residence in the hospital may have been a factor in the attitudes of the future novelist. The building itself was grim; the wing occupied by the family of the chief-of-staff faced a courtyard in which patients sat or walked. The spectacle of illness and suffering was constantly before the child. Flaubert relates how he and Caroline used to pull themselves up to the window of the morgue to look at the bodies awaiting dissection.

The future novelist received the education vouchsafed, in nineteenth-century France, to boys in his social and financial position. In 1832, he entered the *Collège royal de Rouen,* a very distinguished secondary school. Except in history, in which he received several prizes, he was no more than an average student. His love of literature, however, was evident. The assigned reading was, in considerable part, in the classics. If Flaubert failed to distinguish himself in class, he nonetheless left the *lycée* equipped with a substantial Latin culture; he was to read and re-read his favorite Latin authors throughout his life.

More important, and perhaps, more numerous were his voluntary readings in Romantic literature, accomplished under the conditions he was to describe years later:

I don't know what the dreams of school boys are today, but ours were superbly extravagant,—the last expansions of romanticism reaching us —repressed by the provincial environment, created strange turmoils in our brains. . . . We were not only troubadors, insurrectionists, orientals, we were above all artists; the *pensums* done, literature began. We ruined our eyes reading novels in the dormitory. We carried poignards in our pockets like Antony, we did more: out of disgust with existence, Bar[xxx] blew out his brains with a pistol, And [xxx] hanged himself with his necktie. We deserved little praise, certainly, but what hatred of any platitude. What aspirations toward greatness. What respect for the masters. How we admired Victor Hugo.

(*Corr.,* VI, 474)

In the dormitory and during vacations Flaubert read precociously and omnivorously—lyrics, dramas, and novels—and the works of contemporary and medieval historians. Among the authors he mentions most frequently are Goethe, Byron, Shakespeare, Victor Hugo, and, in his last school years, Montaigne, Rabelais, and Ronsard. His Romantic tastes are obvious.

At the age of fourteen he began to compose his own tales and histories. His *Juvenilia,* not all of which have been published, fill three thick volumes. These include dramas such as *Loys XI;* historical narrations such as *La Lutte du Sacerdoce et de l'Empire* (1093-1125); grotesque fantasies like *Ivre et Mort;* and works of pessimistic philosophical pretension like *Rêve d'Enfer* and *Smarh, vieux mystère*. The autobiographical essays, *Mémoires d'un fou* and *Novembre*, testify to the boredom and disdain aroused by classroom and study hall, the extravagance of his dreams, his disgust with the mediocrity of his surroundings, and his aspiration toward a vague but magnificent ideal.

The two friends who had participated in the billiard-table theater were also present at the *collège*. The importance of the first of these, Alfred Le Poittevin, is considerable. He was five years older than Flaubert, and the future novelist admired him, perhaps extravagantly. It is probable that the older student led the younger to questions that he would not yet have asked unguided, that it was under Alfred's influence that Flaubert began to think in philosophical terms, and that his disgust with life, his hatred of the bourgeoisie, and his precocious skepticism about the possibility of happiness derive, in no small part, from this friend. The two men remained intimate until the latter's early death in 1848; to him, Flaubert dedicated the *Mémoires d'un fou* and the *Tentation de Saint-Antoine*. He always spoke with reverence of his literary and metaphysical genius.

Ernest Chevalier, the other great confidant of Flaubert's adolescence, is much less important although he shared the future novelist's literary convictions. It was Flaubert who dominated here, and the intimacy between the two dissolved in Paris, where Chevalier abandoned his schoolboy enthusiasms and went stolidly about the business of building himself a career in the bourgeois world of the law. Although Louis Bouilhet, the great friend of Flaubert's maturity, was also a student at the *collège* during these years, the intimacy between the two men did not begin until 1846.

2.

"Ô chère Trouville"

The Flauberts owned extensive land in the Deauville-Trouville area, and the family was accustomed to spend the summer vacation on the beach at Trouville—then an unspoiled fishing village and not the fashionable resort it was shortly to become. There was the sea and the beach (Flaubert was a fanatical swimmer), there were walks and horseback rides along the dunes, there was boating on the Toucques, and there were pleasant contacts with the local people and with the handful of resorters who returned season after season. In later years, the memory of the summers at Trouville became an obsession for the novelist. The village was, in his mind, the symbol of the golden days of the past when youth hoped and when life was fair.

It was not wholly the sea and dunes which cast this nostalgic charm. Trouville was also the scene of the important emotional experiences of his life. In the summer of 1836, when Flaubert was fourteen and one-half years old, the breath-taking arrival of Madame Maurice Schlésinger brought him the revelation of love. The story probably unfolded much as Flaubert told it in the *Mémoires d'un fou*. The lady, beautiful but above all strange—as Maxime Du Camp described her—with her big dark eyes, her hair in bandeaux, her brownish skin, and her mature, buxom figure appeared on the beach before the bedazzled schoolboy. This passion was to be the torture and the joy of his adolescence. Elisa Schlésinger was the great love of his life. She dominates his work. She is the Maria of the *Mémoires d'un fou,* she is present in *Novembre,* she is Madame Renaud in the first *Education sentimentale.* She is the Emma Bovary, who, at Yonville, repulses the timid advances of Léon. It is possible that she is not absent from certain scenes in *Salammbô. Telle qu'en elle-même enfin,* she receives her supreme incarnation as the touching Madame Arnoux of the definitive *Education.*

Elisa Foucault was born at Vernon in 1810—she was twenty-six years old when Flaubert first saw her at Trouville. The schoolboy did not know (did he ever learn?) that at nineteen she had married an army officer, Emile Judée; had left him for reasons about which we know nothing; and, as there was no divorce in the France of Louis-Philippe, the Maurice Schlésinger with whom she was living was not, in 1836, her husband; and, consequently, the six-months-old child at her breast, the little Marie, was of illegitimate birth. The situation was made regular only after Judée's death in 1839, for the couple married in 1840. Maurice Schlésinger was a Prussian Jew established in Paris where he directed an important music publishing firm and edited a periodical called *la Gazette musicale.*

Through the weeks of this enchanted summer, the infatuated boy observed and worshipped secretly his new-found idol. Fall came; the Schlésingers returned to Paris; Flaubert, to Rouen and school. It is possible—but in my opinion not probable (there may have been other summers on the beach, but we are not informed) —that they did not meet again until Flaubert went to Paris in 1842. But the dream of Madame Schlésinger haunted Flaubert's adolescence. She had become the incarnation and the symbol of all one could hope for in love.

Two things are significant here. The first is the emotional precocity of the boy. His imagination fired beyond his experience by the forced draughts of his reading, and stimulated perhaps by his close association with the nineteen-year-old Le Poittevin, he was able at the age of fourteen to conceive a lasting passion. The second is that he should have found his ideal in a woman he believed to be absolutely unattainable (for the fourteen-year-old boy, of course, she was). Since the only love worth having could not be realized in this world, he was relieved of the responsibility of seeking and of acting. It is possible, too, that he was never afterward able to associate love and fulfillment.

3.

"Qu'est devenu ce bon cabinet de la Gazette musicale, *où l'on disait de si fortes choses entre quatre et six heures du soir?"*

In August, 1840, Flaubert completed his baccalaureate degree. As a compensation, his family arranged for him to take a trip in the company of their friends Dr. Cloquet and his wife; it was to include the Pyrenees, the Mediterranean coast of France, and Corsica. Until now, Flaubert had traveled only from Normandy to Champagne and back again. The sunlight of Provence, the blue of the Mediterranean stimulated his taste for antiquity and his dream of the Orient.

It was time to choose a career. Flaubert's only interest was literature; under pressure from his family, however, he agreed to study law. A full year passed before he registered for the first time at the law school; then, for some months, he continued to live at home, confident that he could prepare for the first-year examination alone. He neglected the law during these months, but he read voraciously, studied Greek, and composed, probably, the first two parts of *Novembre*. He made a prolonged visit to Paris in April, 1842; and at the end of June, he found a room on the Left Bank and at last began attending courses.

Flaubert's career as a law student in Paris lasted, with time out for vacations, until January, 1844, approximately eighteen months. His life was very similar to that of Frederic Moreau in the first part of the *Education sentimentale*. Flaubert's letters groan with complaints about law school—the barbarous Latin, the dullness of the lectures, the stupidity of the subject matter. He passed the first examination in December, 1842, but failed the second in August, 1843.

In March, 1843, he met Maxime Du Camp. The sympathy was immediate, for they had common literary ambitions and common tastes. For ten years Du Camp was to be Flaubert's intimate, his literary confidant, and his traveling companion in Brittany and the Near East. There was coolness between the two in the early 1850's for Flaubert was distressed by Du Camp's efforts to win success by intrigue and publicity rather than by responsible artistry. It was Du Camp, however, who published *Madame Bovary* in the *Revue de Paris* (as he had earlier published Bouilhet); and the friendship between him and Flaubert survived their quarrel and lasted until the latter's death. Du Camp's *Souvenirs littéraires*, published the following year, made revelations about Flaubert's health that seemed indiscreet and in bad taste. The superior and protective tone he adopts toward his deceased friend is irritating. The work must be read with extreme caution, but it remains one of our basic sources of information about Flaubert. From 1843 until 1851, the intimacy with Du Camp was an important factor in the novelist's life and thought.

But above all, in Paris, Flaubert renewed his acquaintance with Madame Schlésinger. The cordiality with which the music publisher welcomed the student and the rapidity with which the younger man established close relations with the older man and his family suggests that there had been contacts more recent than the summer of 1836. Very quickly, Flaubert became a regular guest in the Schlésinger apartment and a habitué of the editorial offices of the *Gazette musicale*. Once again, he was in the presence of his idol.

Elisa Schlésinger, now thirty-two years old, had lost none of her beauty and charm. But Flaubert was no longer fourteen. He seems to have been drawn to Schlésinger, to have been fascinated by his conviviality and aplomb. Flaubert soon became aware, however, of the essential vulgarity and indelicacy of the man, of his multiple marital infidelities, and of the incompatibilities existing between him and his wife. The idol, perhaps, was not so unattainable after all. At any rate, Flaubert tried.

Twenty years ago, Flaubert scholars believed with near unanimity that the relationship had remained platonic, that Madame Schlésinger had been moved by the student's devotion, but that she had refused to yield. In other words, scholars believed that the definitive *Education sentimentale* tells the essential truth. New evidence and a more careful evaluation of the old leave us much less sure today; we shall probably never know what really happened. There is a tempting hypothesis, and I sketch it—fully aware of how highly conjectural it is.

The law student's emotional life was complicated during these months. At the end of the summer of 1842, Flaubert left Paris and the Schlésingers to join his parents on the beach at Trouville. There he met the Collier girls, Gertrude and Harriet, who were spending the summer with their parents at the beach. Their father was an English naval officer who had retired and settled in Paris some years before. When Gustave arrived at the resort, Caroline was already on close terms with the sisters. Harriet was suffering from an undiagnosed ailment and became, at Trouville, the patient of Dr. Flaubert. When the summer ended, the Colliers took hotel rooms in Rouen, so that the physician could continue his treatment. Through September and October, the girls were intimate in the Flaubert household. Early in November, the Colliers returned to their apartment on the Champs-Élysée, and Gustave Flaubert to the Left Bank and to law school. For the rest of his residence in Paris, he was a frequent caller at the Colliers. He was to keep in contact with the girls throughout his life.

There is no doubt that Flaubert's sensibilities were deeply

stirred by Gertrude Collier. Indeed, there is evidence that in November he was seriously considering marrying her. It is interesting to speculate on the difference it would have made to literature if he had yielded to this temptation. We cannot help thinking of the incident in the second part of the definitive *Education sentimentale* in which Frédéric, exhausted and exasperated by Madame Arnoux' refusal to listen, does not reject completely the suggestion that he marry Louise Roque. He goes home to Nogent, and almost without realizing it, finds himself engaged in courtship. Madame Arnoux learns of the proposed marriage, reveals her jealousy, and thus initiates a new phase in her relationship with Frédéric.

There is reason to wonder whether something of the sort did not happen in real life: whether Flaubert did not leave Paris in August, 1842, despondent over his inability to move Madame Schlésinger. At Trouville and later, he experienced a normal attraction to a girl his own age and was tempted by the possibility of marriage. Did Elisa learn of this flirtation with Gertrude? Was there a jealous reaction on her part? Was there a rendezvous, or perhaps an unkept rendezvous like the one that occurs in both versions of the *Education sentimentale?* We may only conjecture.

4.

"J'ai fait de grands progrès tout à coup; et autre chose est venu."

In December, 1843, Flaubert spent Christmas with the Colliers in Paris and New Year's Eve with the Schlésingers at Vernon. He then returned to Rouen for what was to have been a short vacation with his family. A few days later, riding in a carriage with his brother on the road to Pont l'Evêque, he suffered a seizure that marked the onset of a nervous affliction which plagued him the rest of his life. Physicians and biographers who have studied the symptoms are unable to agree on a diagnosis; some believe, as did certain of Flaubert's acquaintances, that it was epilepsy; the novelist called it "my nervous disease." Persons who reject the hypothesis of epilepsy fall back on such vague terms as nervous hysteria. In any case, he was subject to seizures. These ceased, or became very infrequent, after the trip to the Orient of 1849-51; but they struck again in the 1870's at the time of his financial difficulties.

The first attack of this illness marks the end of Flaubert's active life. With the approval of his family, he abandoned the study of law. From this time forward, he devoted himself wholly to literature. In the spring of 1844, his father bought the estate at Croisset. In June, the family took possession of the place, and the life of the hermit began. As he wrote two years later in a letter to Louise Colet:

> He who lives now, and is I, only contemplates the other, who is dead. I have had two entirely distinct existences. Exterior events were the symbol of the end of the first and the birth of the second; all that is mathematical. My active life, passionate, moved, full of leaps in all directions and of multiple sensations, ended when I was twenty-two. At that period, I suddenly made great progress; and something else happened.   (*Corr.*, I, 277 f)

The nervous illness is, as the quotation suggests, much more the symbol than the cause of Flaubert's abandonment of the life of action for the life of meditation and artistic creation. The first seizures only hastened an evolution which was well under way before the end of the Paris days. Flaubert had already determined to live without a profession. He had resisted the impulse to marry Gertrude Collier. As he puts it, he had made important progress. The "external events," the "something else," simply brought things dramatically to a head and created a sharp cleavage between the two phases of his life. Henceforth, he was a spectator and not an actor in this world. In the legendary study at Croisset, everything was to be subordinate to the creation of his work.

Just before, during, and just after the Paris years, Flaubert composed three autobiographical works. The first of these, the *Mémoires d'un fou* describes the ravages and the failure of the protagonist-author's love for Maria-Elisa Schlésinger. The date of its composition is uncertain, but it was probably begun in 1838, although very recent evidence seems to indicate that parts of it could not have been written before 1842. In this case, the longing and despair of the concluding chapters are relevant to the Paris period and reveal something of the emotional disarray of the student.

The second, *Novembre,* composed in 1841 and 1842, tells the story of a romantic dreamer who dies because he cannot adapt to the conditions of life in this world: "Finally, last December, he died, but slowly, little by little, by the force of thought alone, without any organ being ill, as one dies of sadness." (*Oeuvres de Jeunesse,* II, 256) The death of this protagonist symbolizes the end of Flaubert's youth, the end of his personal participation in life.

The *Education sentimentale* (the version of 1845) was begun in Paris in 1843 but was written for the most part in 1844, after the author was stricken. It analyzes the contrasting developments of two young men whose longings and aspirations appear, at the beginning of the story, to be identical. Henry, after a successful intrigue with a woman older than himself, adjusts quickly to active life and is, at the end, well on the way to a substantial position in the world. Jules experiences a disappointment in love, withdraws more and more from life, and finds salvation and serenity in a doctrine of impersonal artistic contemplation and creation. He has become, at the end, "a great and grave artist," and is about to leave for the Orient, taking along a copy of Homer to read on the Hellespont.

Jean Bruneau has defined the significance of these writings: "The internal criticism of *Novembre* and the first *Education sentimentale* shows clearly the deep change that was effected in Flaubert between 1842 and 1845. *Novembre* is still turned toward the past as the dénouement of the novel, the death of the hero, proves. The first *Education sentimentale,* to the contrary, ends with Jules' resolution to begin seriously his labor as an artist. The outlooks of the two novels are thus completely opposed; one considers only the human destiny of the hero, the other transcends man to emerge in Art. With the hero of *Novembre,* Flaubert's youth dies; with the *Education sentimentale* (version of 1845) his maturity begins." [1]

CHAPTER 4

Saint Anthony

1.

"C'est l'oeuvre de toute ma vie"

ON March 3, 1845, Caroline Flaubert married her brother's school companion, Emile Hamard. The family accompanied the newly-weds on their honeymoon in Italy. At Genoa, in May, the future novelist saw Breughel's painting, "The Temptation of Saint Anthony," and he formed the ambitious plan to adapt the subject to the theater. He returned to Croisset in June, meditating the project that was to occupy him intermittently unil 1874. He immediately began the reading and research necessary to the realization of his conception.

But life at Croisset was troubled. In January, 1846, Dr. Flaubert died of a phlegmon in his thigh. In February, Caroline Hamard gave birth to the little Caroline who, as Madame Commanville, and later, as Madame Franklin-Grout, was to be the novelist's literary executor and the owner of his papers. In March, the mother died of puerperal fever, and Hamard entrusted the baby to the care of her grandmother. The household at Croisset—Madame Flaubert, little Caroline, and the servant Julie—in which the novelist's life would center for many years came into being.

These months saw only the beginning of the intimacy between Flaubert and his former school mate, Louis Bouilhet, the great friend and the most important literary confidant of his maturity. Bouilhet had abandoned the study of medicine to devote himself to literature. A position as tutor in a Rouen school provided him with a mean living. He shared Flaubert's esthetic doctrine and artistic integrity. From 1846 forward, Bouilhet spent countless week-ends at Croisset, where the two men talked, read, wrote, and criticized each other's work. Bouilhet became the novelist's *alter ego* and literary conscience. A minor poet and not very successful playwright, Bouilhet was not Flaubert's peer, but the latter had complete confidence in his esthetic judgment. His friendship with Flaubert is his greatest claim to glory. With his appearance at Croisset in 1846, the environment in which the novelist worked assumed its final form.

In Paris that summer for a visit, Flaubert met Louise Colet, and began what was to be a long and stormy liaison. The relationship was broken off in 1848, resumed in 1851 and continued until 1855. Madame Colet, a beautiful woman, was a poet of little talent. She was a well-known and sometimes notorious figure in literary circles in the capital. There is no reason to discuss the details of this affair, for Flaubert was determined to keep it subordinate to what he believed to be the exigencies of his literary vocation. His sentimental education was already complete, and Madame Colet could have no real influence on him. As he wrote her with an honesty that skirted tactlessness, "For me, love is not and must not be in the foreground of life; it must remain in the wings. There are other things ahead of it in the soul, which are, it seems to me, nearer to light, closer to the sun. If, therefore, you treat love as the main course in life: NO. As a relish: YES." (*Corr.*, II, 19) Remarks like this did little to calm relationships with the demanding and vehement Louise. Nor did Flaubert's refusal to live with her in Paris and his insistence that he could pursue his vocation only in the calm of Croisset. To the distance which separated them, however, we owe the remarkable series of letters which he wrote two to three times a week through 1847 and 1848 and from 1851 to 1855. Herein lies, for us, the real importance of this affair. The letters contain the most striking statements of Flaubert's esthetic doctrine. Through them we can follow, almost page by page, the composition of *Madame Bovary*.

The occupation which kept Flaubert at Rouen and far from Paris and Louise Colet was the creation of the earliest version of the *Temptation of Saint Anthony*. After months of reading and research, composition was begun in May, 1848. Seventeen months later, in September, 1849, the bulky manuscript was complete. The speed and apparent facility with which Flaubert wrote this huge work contrast sharply with the slow and laborious elaboration of the novels that he was to produce in the future. He thought that at last he had accomplished something good. In high enthusiasm, he summoned Bouilhet and Du Camp to Croisset to hear him read his creation, a reading which must have been an ordeal for the two auditors. It lasted thirty-two hours. "For four days," according to Du Camp, "Flaubert read without intermission from noon until four o'clock and from eight o'clock until midnight." After the last session, "Towards midnight, Flaubert, pounding on the table, said to us 'Among the three of us now, tell me frankly what you think.' Bouilhet was timid, but no one appeared firmer than he in the expression of his thought when he had decided to make it known. He answered: 'We think that you must burn that, and never speak about it again.'" [1]

Flaubert staggered under the blow. He believed in his work; he likewise trusted and believed in his chosen judges. He accepted the sentence and eventually yielded to his friends' advice that he undertake a homely, familiar subject in which lyric digressions would be absurd. But he did not burn his manuscript. In 1856, after the completion of *Madame Bovary*, he pulled it out of his drawers and rewrote it; he reduced its length by almost one-half and was prepared to publish the revised version when the prosecution of *Madame Bovary* made the venture seem inexpedient. For fourteen years more, while Flaubert engaged in other labors, the manuscripts lay in the drawers at Croisset while the idea worked on in the author's mind. Between 1870 and 1872, the composition was completely recast, revised, and again reduced in length. It is the last and definitive version which was published in 1874. Understandably, the author referred to it as "the book of my whole lifetime."

2.

"Messieurs les démons, quittez-moi donc."

The *Tentation de Saint-Antoine* does not lend itself easily to formal classification. It is a loose dramatic monologue, a prose poem with encyclopedic philosophical and historical intentions. It is also a dream, or better yet an hallucination, and a catalogue and evocation of all the mythologies which have shaped the dreams of

[52]

mankind. It was partly inspired by *Faust* and is often compared
to the German masterpiece; but, as Harry Levin has pointed out,
Faust's quest for many-sided fulfillment has little in common with
the agonized renunciation of Flaubert's lonely, ascetic hero. Ed-
gar Quinet's all but forgotten symbolical work *Ahasvérus,* treating
the legend of the Wandering Jew, which Flaubert read in the
1830's, also served as a model.

The historical Anthony was the earliest of the monks and the
leader of the ascetic movement in the Egypt of the fourth century.
It is noteworthy that Flaubert should have treated, in time, the
moment of convergence between Paganism and Christianity and,
in space, the point of contact between East and West. The multiple forms assumed by religion, civilization, and life, one merging
with the other, parade before the bewildered eyes of the belea-
guered, passive protagonist. Sanctity is colored by sensuality, Lust
embraces Death, Christian rites become abominations of serpent
worship; and, everywhere, everything is degenerating and passing
away. "The Holy of Holies is open; the veil is torn," mourns the
Lord of Hosts. The question which Anthony asks, at the end of
the work, before the profusion of animal life, "But if substance is
unique, why should Forms be varied?" is implied in each of the
hallucinations of the agonizing night of temptation.

The scene opens with Anthony alone before his hut, high on a
mountain, overlooking the Nile and the desert, with the Libyan
Mountains in the distance. The sun is setting. He is weary of making baskets and mats; his desire to pray—his happiness in devotion—have dried up; he has doubts about his vocation. He recalls
his childhood, his home, his mother, his sweetheart, his decision to
adopt the anchoret's life, and his early days as a monk. Birds of
passage flying overhead make him long to join them. He medi-
tates on other lives he might have led, other careers he might have
made—parish priest, philosopher, soldier, merchant, farmer with
wife and children. His discouragement is complete: "What solitude, what tedium. *Laughing bitterly.* This is a fine existence,
twisting palm sticks in the fire to make shepherds' crooks, shaping
baskets, sewing mats, then trading all that to Nomads for bread
which breaks one's teeth. Ah, alas for me. Will it never end?
Death would be better. I can't go on. Enough, enough." (8)

In an effort to get hold of himself, Anthony begins to read his

Bible. The passages on which he falls suggest feasting, carnage, and vengeance, orgy, wealth, and, in the visit of the Queen of Sheba to Solomon, carnal love. Unable to control his imagination and weak from fasting, Anthony becomes faint. The scene ends with a striking description of the onset of hallucination, inspired by the author's experiences in his nervous seizures: "Despite the tumult in his head, he perceives an enormous silence which separates him from the world. He tries to speak; impossible. It is as if the whole organization of his being were dissolving; and, no longer resisting, Anthony falls on the mat." (15)

It should be noted that all of the dreams which follow derive from Anthony's meditations in this first scene—many details of which have necessarily been omitted here—or from the readings from the Bible. In this final version of the *Temptation*, Flaubert has abandoned most of the medieval trappings of the earlier manuscripts, and he has endeavored to describe scientifically the onset of catalepsy and hallucination in a monk maddened by loneliness and weakened by privation and mortification.

The second scene is closely bound to the first. Anthony, in his visions, is tempted by rich, rare, and abundant food—and by wealth beyond all earthly need. He enters Alexandria and partakes in the massacre of the Arians. At Byzantium, he is honored by the emperor; he delights in an orgy with Nebuchadnezzer, and wakens before his own hut. In penitence for his dreams, he scourges himself with his discipline, thinks of his sweetheart Ammonaria, and is visited and tempted by the Queen of Sheba and her retinue: "I am not a woman, I am a world. My clothes have only to fall, and you will discover on my person a succession of mysteries." (36) Anthony refuses, and the queen and her slaves disappear.

We have passed rapidly over these scenes because the great temptations, for Anthony, are not the pomps and vanities of this wicked world, nor yet the sinful lusts of the flesh. The thirst for knowledge is far more dangerous. In the earlier versions, the seven deadly sins, to whom only passing reference is made in the definitive work, are accompanied by an eighth named Logic. In the final form, Logic's role is assumed by Anthony's former pupil, Hilarion, who is mentioned in the first scene, and who appears after the departure of the Queen of Sheba. Hilarion grows larger with each succeeding episode and finally reveals himself as Science. He first challenges Anthony's vocation and way of life.

Hypocrite, who flounders in solitude, better to savour the overflow of his lusts. You do without meat, wine, baths, slaves, and honors; but how you let your imagination offer you banquets, perfumes, naked women, and applauding crowds. Your chastity is only a more subtle corruption and this scorn of the world only the impotence of your hatred for it. That's what makes men like you so lugubrious, or perhaps the fact that they doubt. The possession of truth brings joy. Was Jesus sad? . . .

ANTHONY

breaks into tears. (42)

Hilarion proposes to introduce Anthony to sages who will unveil for him the face of the Unknown; and then the long parade of heresiarchs, false prophets, and magicians begins. This procession occupies sixty-six pages in the Conard text of the work (it was much longer in the earlier versions). Mani and Valentinus, Montanus and Origen, Arius and Sabellus appear in their costumes and expound their doctrines to the saint. We are introduced to Caprocanists, Apollinarists, Marcionites, Cainites, and a profusion of others too numerous to mention. When the saint asks "What is the Word? What was Jesus?," the babel of conflicting definition and contradictory doctrine becomes bewildering. At last:

ANTHONY

briskly, raises his head, looks at them without speaking; then walking straight toward them:
Doctors, magicians, bishops and deacons, men and fantomes, behind, behind me. You are all lies.

THE HERESIARCHS

We have martyrs more martyr than yours, more difficult prayers, superior outbursts of love, ecstasies just as long.

ANTHONY

But no revelation. No proof
Then, all brandish in the air rolls of papyrus, tablets of wood, pieces of leather, strips of cloth;—and pushing each other: (70)
each reveals his gospel.

[55]

Three hallucinations now lay bare corruptions of piety. Anthony witnesses a ceremony in which the rites of the church are mocked in worship of a serpent. Christian martyrs, about to enter the arena, look longingly at this life and curse a heretic who shares their fate. In a cemetery, survivors who have come to mourn their martyrs indulge in sexual orgy between the tombstones.

A gymnosophist, as the flames of his pyre converge around him, proclaims the teachings of Indian asceticism. Simon the Magician appears, accompanied by an Ennoia, who has been Helen of Troy, Delilah, Lucretia, and countless other women. Finally Apollonius of Tyana arrives and, in a long dialogue, offers to reveal to Anthony the secrets of the gods. Anthony clings to his cross, the vision disappears, and the long scene of the false prophets and magicians ends.

But the saint would like to know the gods; Hilarion, ever present, obliges, and a veritable Götterdämmerung presents itself before their eyes. One after the other, the religions of all mankind appear and state their claims. First, there are the almost amorphous idols of the most primitive tribes. Bit by bit, however, the divinities assume human forms. The gods of the Brahmins occupy the landscape; the Buddha tells his story, elaborates his conception of life and the universe, and announces the destruction of the worlds. The Chaldean, Babylonian, Persian, and Syrian divinities proclaim their legends and their rites, and pass into oblivion. Isis relates her union with the dead Osiris, regrets her vanished Egypt, and disappears with a piercing cry as Harpocrates dies. Mount Olympus appears, and a palace of bronze with golden tiles and ivory capitals is peopled by the classical gods: "How beautiful it is," exclaims Anthony, and Hilarion, impassive Science though he be, reveals an enthusiasm that suggests that Flaubert, too, was moved:

They leaned from the top of the clouds to direct the swords. One met them on the roadsides, one possessed them in the house—and that familiarity lent divinity to life.

Its only purpose was to be free and beautiful. Loose clothes facilitated the nobility of attitudes. The voice of the orator, trained by the sea, beat in sonorous waves against the marble porticoes. The ephebe, rubbed with oil, wrestled naked in full sunlight. The most religious action was to expose pure forms.

And these men respected matrons, the aged, supplicants. Behind the temple of Hercules, there was an altar to Pity.

They sacrificed victims with flowers around their fingers. Memory itself was exempt from the decay of the dead. All that remained of them was a little bit of ash. The soul, mingled with the limitless ether, had gone off toward the gods. (148)

The temptation is almost too much to resist. But Anthony recites his creed, the cross casts its shadow over the palace, and one after the other the Olympians pale, stagger, and fall.

A succession of minor gods now take the stage, including the perhaps aprocryphal Crepitus, who is treated with the same dignity accorded Buddha or Jupiter. Then at last a voice thunders:

I was the Lord of Hosts, the Lord, the Lord God. I unfolded Jacob's tents on the Hills, and fed my fleeing people in the sands.

It is I who burned Sodom. It is I who buried the earth under the Flood. It is I who drowned Pharaoh, with the princes sons of kings, the war chariots and the drivers. . . . The Holy of Holies is open, the veil is torn. . . . my people is dispersed. (165)

The voice fades in the distance leaving "an enormous silence, a profound night."

"All have passed," says Anthony.
"I remain,"
　　says

SOMEONE

and Hilarion is before him, but transfigured fair
as an archangel, shining as a sun,—and so large,
that to see him

ANTHONY

throws back his head.
Who are you then?

HILARION

My kingdom is the dimension of the universe, and my desire has no limits. I go forward always, freeing minds and weighing worlds, without hatred, without pity, without love, and without God. I am called Science.   (166)

We must note two things about this parade of the religions. The first is that, with nearly every manifestation, Hilarion points out the similarities between the other faiths and the Christian belief of Anthony. The three-headed god in the chalice of the lotus of the Brahmins suggests the Trinity. Hilarion takes pains to indicate the parallels between the life of Buddha and the life of Christ. In an intermission between the appearances of the gods, Anthony thinks with pity of all the souls lost by these false divinities. "Don't you think," replies Hilarion, "that they have resemblances to the true?" (145)

The second is the constant flow and metamorphosis of forms and phenomena. As in a kaleidoscope, there is a constant passage from one pattern to the next; as on a screen, a picture appears out of an unfocused blur, and in turn blurs away to give place to the picture that will follow. One god pushes and destroys the next. Everything is degenerating and passing away. The forms are constantly changing, yet merge one with another. The substance is unique, but why are the forms in constant and never ending flux?

The Devil (or is it Hilarion?) now takes Anthony into the heavens and shows him, not the kingdoms of this world, but the countless millions of worlds. The saint falls back to the earth with a shudder before "the eternal silence of infinite space." "Good and evil concern you alone—like day and night, pleasure and pain, birth and death, which are relative to a corner of space, to a special environment, to a peculiar interest. Since infinity alone is permanent, there is the Infinite;—and that is all." (175)

The dialogue between Death and Lust and their sisterly embrace now make manifest to Anthony the antithesis, dear to Flaubert, of creation and destruction, generation and dissolution, the carnal and charnel, and the persistence of life through the metamorphosis of its forms: "Thus death is only an illusion, a veil, masking, here and there, the continuity of life." (187) The impossibility of the union of the Sphinx and Chimera incarnates the impotence of Fantasy and Imagination: their inability to cope with the unknown.

A series of fantastic and legendary monsters, drawn apparently

from medieval bestiaries, now appears. Anthony shudders in be-
wilderment before the profusion and proliferation of life in all its
multiple forms: mammals, serpents, insects, birds, and at last the
creatures of the sea. The animal world merges into the vegetal,
and the plants are indistinguishable from the stones. The saint
throws himself on the earth to watch the proliferating protozoa
and experiences the supreme temptation:

Joy, joy. I have seen life begin, I have seen movement commence.
The blood in my veins beats so hard that it is going to burst them.
I feel like flying, swimming, barking, bellowing, roaring. I should
like to have wings, a shell, a bark, to breathe smoke, to swing a trunk,
to twist my body, to divide everywhere, to be in everything, to ema-
nate with the odors, to develop like the plants, to flow like water,
vibrate like sound, shine like light, to creep into all the forms, penetrate every atom, descend to the depth of matter,—to be matter. (200)

Day appears at last. The face of Jesus Christ shines in the disk of
the sun, and Anthony resumes his prayers.

3.

*"Mais la substance étant unique, pourquoi les Formes sont-elles
variées?"*

The *Tentation de Saint-Antoine* is a stupendous accomplishment, but not, even in the final version, without its weaknesses.
Interest lags in spots, particularly in the parade of the heresies,
which is too long and too lacking in variety. If Flaubert's intention
was to offer a picture of the fourth-century mind, shaped by the
decline of a classical culture and the rise of Catholicism, influenced by the thought patterns of the East and West, he was not
wholly successful. As Taine observed in a letter congratulating the
author, the science and philosophy of the last scenes of the work
were beyond the scope of the awareness of the founder of monas-
ticism. Because of the nature of the subject, there can be little
action and less drama. Out of necessity, the protagonist is passive
and a spectator.

But the psychological aspects of the story are handled convincingly and skillfully. The apparitions develop logically from the thoughts and reminiscences of the saint; the forms they take are determined by his experience; the mechanisms of hallucination are clearly indicated, and one vision leads naturally to the next. It is here, perhaps, that the definitive version is most superior to the earlier manuscripts.

The myths, dreams, and aspirations of humanity, the whole drama of mankind endeavoring to understand its destiny is presented, not only in the sonorous dialogue, but also in the clearly visualized plasticity of the images. To set them down accurately, Flaubert apprehended the culture of venerable traditions and submitted to a severe discipline of study and research. The erudition which he brought to his dream is overwhelming—too much so perhaps for most readers.

In the final version, the bewildering multiplicity of the dreams and the nightmares is depicted and presented with consummate art. One is often reminded of a surrealistic film; strange and striking images blend and merge, one into the other; forms dissolve; everything is decaying and passing to oblivion. Yet new forms constantly appear. The reader, like the saint, staggers, intoxicated by the eternal metamorphosis of the hearts and minds of men and the myths by which they live; of the stars that burn out, yet are formed anew in the infinite emptiness of space; of the alternation of life and death in their myriad forms in the adventure of protoplasm on this earth.

In *The Gates of Horn*, Harry Levin has entitled his discussion of the *Temptation* "The Martyrdom of St. Polycarp." [2] Flaubert identified himself with this father of the church, the burden of whose complaint was the degeneracy of the age and the land in which God had called him to live. In an earlier form, this essay carried the even more telling title: "Portrait of the Artist as a Saint." In any case, there is perhaps more of Flaubert in Saint Anthony than in any other of his characters. The abnegation, discipline, and contemplation of the saint on his mountain top have their counterpart in the laborious life of the hermit of Croisset. Despite temptations and nightmares, despite the doubts that sneered in his face, the artist, like the saint, persevered. He was convinced that he was in the right and that what he was doing was good, that the ordeal would end with dawn; and, in the disk of the sun, Truth apprehended through Beauty would shine forth. And, as Mr. Levin has pointed out, Anthony lived to confound the Arians and gave aid and comfort to the faithful.

CHAPTER 5

Triumph

1.

"Il voyagea."

SHORTLY after the disastrous reading in September, 1849, of the first *Tentation de Saint-Antoine*, Flaubert and Du Camp set off on a twenty-one-month trip through the Near East. In April, Flaubert had been advised by his doctor to travel in warm climes. Du Camp had already conceived the then novel idea of making a travel book with photographs of Egypt and Asia Minor. He suggested that Flaubert accompany him; the latter was over-joyed and asked only that the departure be postponed until he could complete the *Tentation*.

The friends, accompanied by a servant, sailed from Marseille on November 4th. After a visit to Alexandria, and a stay of more than two months in Cairo, with excursions to the Pyramids and Memphis, they went up the Nile into upper Egypt on a chartered cangia. This exploration occupied five months; they returned to Cairo on June 26th. In July, they reached Beyrouth; from there they toured the Holy Land. They made their way slowly up the Asia Minor Coast, reaching Constantinople in November. On December 25th, they were in Athens. January was spent touring Greece; February saw them in Italy. They reached Rome, where they were met by Flaubert's mother, on March 28th. Du Camp returned to Paris, but Gustave and Madame Flaubert stayed on until May. They visited Florence, Venice, Cologne, and Brussels before returning to Croisset in June.

All in all, Flaubert was pleased with the trip. He had treated himself to "a bellyful of colors"; he had meditated before the vestiges of the most venerable antiquity; he had seen the Pyramids, the Holy Sepulchre, and the Parthenon. He had brought back careful notes of his observations and impressions. The spectacle of the East, the juxtaposition of color and squalor, nourished his taste for the *grotesque triste;* it likewise reinforced his misanthropy, convincing him that human stupidity and meanness were universal. Years later, he evoked these months in the unforgettable sentences of the *Education sentimentale:* "He traveled. He experienced the melancholy of steamboats, the cold wakenings in the tent, the giddying succession of landscapes and ruins, the bitterness of interrupted sympathies. He came back." (600) His health was improved; he was thirty years old and nearly bald; he had spent on the trip most of the liquid capital of his inheritance from his father.

Throughout his travels Flaubert had meditated on his future literary activities. His friends' condemnation of the *Saint Anthony* had been a shock and a blow to his confidence. In a letter to Bouilhet in September, 1850, he was still thinking about it: "I have none the less recovered (not without difficulty) from the frightful blow that *Saint Anthony* brought me. I do not claim that I am not still a little bit giddy from it, but I am no longer sick about it as I was for the first four months of my trip. I saw everything through the veil of woe in which this disappointment had enveloped me, and I kept repeating the inept words that you now write me: 'What's the use?'" (*Corr.*, II, 237) Two months later, he wrote the same correspondent from Constantinople of his desire to prove himself to himself. He was pondering three subjects: a Don Juan, an Anubis, and the tale of a girl who dies in mystic ecstasy in a Flemish village. He did not mention *Madame Bovary.*

2.

"Je les aurai connues, les affres du style."

At the time of the reading of *Saint Anthony*, the critic-friends had warned Flaubert against the fantasy of his imagination and his tendency to lyric flight. They had suggested that he undertake a domestic drama, like those of Balzac, in which there would be no place for such developments. Du Camp affirms that the Delamare story was discussed that evening. There is, however, no evidence that Flaubert thought about such a book during the trip.

Back in France, in July, 1851, Du Camp interrogated his friend: "What are you doing? What are you deciding? What are you working on? What are you writing? Have you decided? *Is it still Don Juan?* Is it the story of Mme De La Marre which is very beautiful?" [1] The answer to these questions was shortly to be revealed. In September, Flaubert, resolved to tell the story of Delphine Delamare, began work on *Madame Bovary.*

There is no reason to think that Flaubert had ever met his models. He and Bouilhet were familiar, however, at least in outline, with the misfortunes of Eugene Delamare, a decent, dull, plodding fellow who had studied medicine under the novelist's father. He had established a practice in the village of Ry; he had married, first, a woman years older than himself, and then, on her death, Delphine Couturier, the daughter of a prosperous farmer. The second Madame Delamare had two affairs and died in 1848, leaving a little girl and heavy debts. The long tradition that she committed suicide is not supported by any concrete evidence. Her husband followed her in death a few months later.

These few facts provided Flaubert with the outline and plot of his novel. It appears unlikely, however, that he drew any further than this on the Delamare story. The resemblance between Yonville l'Abbaye and Ry consists only in the fact that both are characteristic Norman villages. There is no evidence that Flaubert ever went to Ry; the town is mentioned nowhere in his notes, outlines, or sketches (neither is the name Delamare); the legend which has grown up associating its inhabitants with the personages of the novel is, in all probability, wholly apocryphal.

The real-life Delamare tragedy provided only the outline for the new project. In Flaubert's mind, the subject was closely related to the story of the Flemish mystic which he had pondered in the East. Discussing Emma Bovary, after the publication of the novel, he wrote:

The first idea I had was to make a spinster of her, living out in the provinces, growing old in grief and reaching thus the last stages of mysticism and imaginary passion. I kept from this first plan all the surroundings (landscapes, and rather black characters), the color in a word. Only, to make the story more comprehensible and more amusing, in the good sense of the word, I invented a more human heroine, a woman like those one sees more often. (*Corr.*, IV, 168)

The author modified this plan because it would entail the risk of falling into the errors which had spoiled the earliest *Saint Anthony*. He would again be dealing with a mystic, an exceptional being withdrawn from the normal conditions of life, and he would again be tempted to substitute his own dreams and personality for those of his personage. The artist must look outside himself if he is to apprehend general truth. The neurotic Flaubert was too close to the hallucinations of the frustrated mystic. Emma Bovary would be more normal, more comprehensible, and hence a symbol of more universal validity. And he needed an anchor in reality to curb his imagination. As he wrote Louise Colet shortly after beginning composition: "I am in an entirely different world now, that of attentive observation of the flattest details. I am concentrating my glance on the mildew traces of the soul. It's a far cry from the mythological and theological flamboyancies of *St. Anthony*. And in as much as the subject is different, I am writing with a wholly different method. I want to have in my book not a single movement, not a single reflection of the author." (*Corr.*, II, 365) Thus Flaubert acknowledged the soundness of his friends' strictures on the *Temptation*.

From September, 1851, until early 1856, the composition of *Madame Bovary* occupied the author's every energy. It was during these years that the mature Flaubert, the Flaubert of history, emerged. His apprenticeship was over. Though he had as yet published nothing, he had written thousands of pages, perfected his instruments and techniques, and knew what he was about. Life at Croisset assumed the patterns of the legend: Flaubert, his mother and his niece; work in the lonely study from early afternoon until dinner, and then into the wee hours of the morning; the instruction of little Caroline in the morning (Madame Franklin-Grout says she grew up believing that Bovary meant work and that work meant writing); week-end visits by Louis Bouilhet, when the two writers read together and criticized each other's work. Every three months, more or less, the novelist allowed himself a few days respite and a reunion with Louise Colet, sometimes in Paris, sometimes in the hotel at Mantes.

For the first time, writing became difficult for him; he began the complaint, to be repeated through the composition of every novel, about *les affres du style*. His ideal of style was now so demanding, he was so meticulous in his scruples, that words, sentences, paragraphs, and transitions could be elaborated and contrived only with painful labor and deliberation: "I have been five days writing a page, and I have abandoned everything for that, Greek, English." (*Corr.*, II, 350) Problems of organization, tone, and color were equally distressing:

A book is such a heavy machine to construct, and above all, complicated. What I am writing at present runs the risk of being like Paul de Kock if I don't give it a profoundly literary form. But how to make trivial dialogue which is well written? . . . In a book like this one, a deviation of one line can make me miss the goal completely, make me fail entirely. At the point where I am, the simplest sentence has an infinite bearing on the rest. Hence all the time that I put into it, the rejections, the disgust, the slowness. (*Corr.*, III, 20)

The platitude and meanness of the subject nauseated him; it was impossible to create beauty out of such material; he was engaged on a laborious *pensum*, on a futile exercise in composition; he was like a man trying to play the piano with leaden weights on his fingers. The litany of his complaints was endless.

But he was also challenged by the novelty and the originality of his undertaking. He glimpsed immense possibilities: "The whole value of my book, if it has one, will be to be able to walk straight on a hair suspended between the double abyss of lyricism and vulgarity (which I wish to blend in a narrative analysis). When I think of what that can be I am bedazzled. But when I think that so much beauty has been entrusted to me, I feel pangs of dread which make me want to flee and hide anywhere at all." (*Corr.*, II, 372) There were also moments of joy:

It is a delightful thing to write, to no longer be oneself, but to circulate in the whole creation of which one is speaking. Today, for example, man and woman together, lover and mistress at the same time,

I rode horseback in a forest, on an autumn afternoon, under yellow leaves, and I was the horses, the leaves, the wind. . . . When I ruminate these joys after experiencing them, I would be tempted to offer a prayer of thanks to the good Lord, if I knew that he could hear me. May he be blessed for not having made me a dry goods merchant, a vaudevillist, a wit.   (*Corr.*, III, 405)

And there were triumphs, such as the morning when Flaubert read, in the *Journal de Rouen*'s account of a political harangue, a sentence he had himself, the night before, written for the speech of the prefect at the *Commices agricoles:* "Not only was it the same idea, the same words, but the same assonances of style. I do not hide that things like that please me. When literature attains the precision of an exact science, that's something." (*Corr.*, III, 285) Despite his complaints and moans, despite the *affres du style,* Flaubert knew the satisfaction of vocation and the joy of creation.

In the spring of 1856, Du Camp, now the director of *La Revue de Paris,* agreed to publish his friend's novel in serial form—despite the fact that a marked coolness had developed in 1853 in the relations of the two men. The first installment appeared in October; the sixth and last in December. The Imperial government immediately prosecuted the author and the editors for an offense against civic and religious morality. The motive was probably less pruriency on the part of the authorities than the desire of the government to find an excuse to suppress *La Revue de Paris.* Flaubert and his friends brought powerful influences to bear. They did not succeed in quashing the suit, but a judgment which appeared to say "not guilty, but don't do it again" acquitted the novel and the accused. The publisher Michel Lévy produced the first edition in book form in April, 1857. Success, to which the accusation of immorality contributed not a little, was immediate.

3.

"C'était la faute de la fatalité."

The plot of *Madame Bovary* is so well known it needs only to be traced in barest outline. The novel opens with the arrival at the

Collège de Rouen of Charles Bovary, a gangling, inept, country boy who is the son of a ne'er-do-well father and of a zealous mother. By dint of application, he finishes school; and, after a preliminary failure, he passes his examinations for a medical degree. He begins to practice in the village of Tostes; and, at the urging of his mother, he marries a widow, reputedly rich, but years older than he. When the widow dies suddenly (leaving nothing), he is already in love with the daughter of a patient, the comfortable farmer, Monsieur Rouault, whose broken leg he has set. After a decent interval, Charles woos and wins Emma Rouault.

Emma has been brought up a lady. In her convent school, her senses opened to the mysticism and sensuality of the ritual; she responded to exotic and romantic books; and she dreamed of a life, rich, colorful, and perfumed—and of ineffable expansions of rare and passionate love. She was called upon to live in Tostes in the Norman countryside with the plodding, unimaginative Charles. Early in her marriage, a chance invitation to an aristocratic ball allows her to glimpse the luxurious life of which she has dreamed. Total disillusionment follows, and she persuades her husband to abandon Tostes and to settle in the somewhat larger town of Yonville-l'Abbaye where things must be more as she desires them.

But Yonville is as dreary as Tostes, and Charles is no less dull because of the move. A daughter is born. Emma feels sympathy with a timid and sentimental law clerk, Léon, who reads verse and shares her boredom with country life. An inactive, platonic flirtation follows. Léon goes off to Paris to finish his law studies. Emma is then seduced by Rodolphe, a country gentleman and sport whose experience with women is extensive. The affair palls; Emma dreams of glory as Charles, inspired by the pompous pharmacist, undertakes to operate on the clubfoot of a stable boy. When gangrene develops and the leg must be amputated, Emma, disgusted anew by the ineptitude of her husband, turns back to Rodolphe and urges him to elope with her. He reluctantly agrees but backs out at the last minute in a letter of unconscious cruelty. For weeks Emma lies between life and death, but she slowly recovers. At the end of her convalescence, Charles takes her to the opera at Rouen, where the tenor, Lagardy, singing in *Lucia*, reawakens all the romantic longings of Emma's nature and education. Léon has finished his study in Paris and is now practicing law in Rouen. They meet him at the theater.

The affair with Léon ensues. On various pretexts, Emma arranges to spend one day a week in Rouen where the lovers rent a hotel room in which they can meet whenever she gets to the city. Her passion for Léon, overpowering at first, grows weaker; but she continues out of habit and because her love, unsatisfactory as it is, is all she has left. Her tastes become increasingly extravagant; she squanders money she does not possess. Earlier, in the days of Rodolphe, she had had recourse to the usurer, Lheureux. She continues to call on him and her indebtedness piles up. Lheureux, in due course, forecloses and seizes the Bovarys' household effects. After an hallucinating scene in which Emma endeavors without success to obtain money from her lovers and others, she swallows arsenic and dies. Charles, still deeply in love with her, discovers her letters and dies of grief a few months later. Little Berthe, the daughter, is cared for by impoverished relatives who put her to work in the textile mills.

4.

"Madame Bovary *n'a rien de vrai.*"

This plot follows closely the Delamare story; but, as we have seen, Flaubert seems to have drawn only the plot from the scandal at Ry. The author insisted that the novel was wholly imaginary: "No, sir, no model posed for me. *Madame Bovary* is a pure invention. All the characters in the book are completely products of my imagination, and Yonville-l'Abbaye is a region which does not exist." (*Corr.*, IV, 191) In the real sense he was right—but obviously the picture was influenced by persons he knew, or knew about, and by incidents he had lived through or observed.

Important parts of the novel derive from the adventures of a woman Flaubert knew well, perhaps intimately. Louise Pradier, the wife of the sculptor, found herself after a succession of adulteries, hopelessly in debt and threatened with foreclosure. Her story is related in detail in a document found among Flaubert's papers. Like Emma, Madame Pradier obtained power of attorney from her husband; like Emma, she ran madly to her former lovers in a vain effort to raise enough money to stop the sheriff's sale. Like Charles, her husband knew nothing about the situation until he saw the placard announcing the auction of his property. Madame Pradier considered suicide; but, unlike Emma, she lived on.

In her domineering possessiveness, in the intensity, the vehemence of her feelings, Emma also suggests Louise Colet. The Muse, like the heroine, presented her lover with a signet bearing the inscription *"amor nel cor."* The couple in the hotel room at Rouen has much in common with the pair who enjoyed blissful reunions in the hotel room at Mantes. If, in Rouen, Emma and Léon seem Flaubert and the Muse, in the earlier scene at Yonville they suggest Flaubert and Madame Schlésinger. Lèon's timid, unexpressed love and Emma's reserve behind her domestic occupations were remembered by the author; he recalled them again for use in the *Education sentimentale.* The apprentice apothecary, Justin, lovesick and mute before Emma's beauty, is also strangely reminiscent of the moonstruck adolescent on the beach at Trouville. The competent Dr. Larivière, "practicing virtue without believing in it," is a tribute to the author's father. Certain details of Emma's agony and burial seem to have been suggested by the death of Caroline Flaubert Hamard.

The point is that Flaubert always started from reality. When personal experience and observation were not adequate to the situation, he relied on scrupulous documentation. Thus he read the *Mémoires* of Madame Lafarge, whose trial for the murder of her husband intrigued France in 1840. This woman's story does not resemble Madame Bovary's, but her temperament and the intensity of her indignation and disgust with her uninspiring husband seem very close to Emma's.

To give specific form to his heroine's youthful dreams, the novelist studied the *Keepsakes* that fascinated nineteenth-century schoolgirls. Before writing the scene in which Rodolphe courts Emma at the *Commices agricoles,* he spent a day with Bouilhet at one of these county fairs. He cross-examined his physician brother about clubfeet; and, apparently not sure that he understood, he studied a medical treatise on the subject before describing the operation. This documentation and his personal experience provide the particulars—the concrete reality which he proceeds to transmute into general truth. The drama at Ry, the lovers at

Mantes, or Caroline dying in childbirth, transcend their personal, relative, and ephemeral nature and become symbols of universal validity: "Everything that we invent is true; be sure of it. Poetry is just as precise as geometry. Induction is quite as good as deduction, and then, when one reaches a certain point, one no longer makes mistakes about anything that concerns the soul. My poor Bovary, doubtless, is suffering and weeping in twenty villages in France at the same time, at this very hour." (*Corr.*, III, 291)

The sources, the roots in reality, personal and documentary, are there. If we want to, we can find them. But it is worse than misleading to suggest, as some commentators have appeared to do, that Flaubert was telling the story of Madame Delamare, or of Madame Pradier. Even less was he trying to narrate his own sentimental involvements.

5.

"Ma pauvre Bovary, sans doute, souffre et pleure dans vingt villages de France à la fois, à cette heure même."

The universal truth for which Flaubert was reaching is expressed most explicitly, perhaps, in a passage which occurs in the second part of the novel. Rodolphe, who thinks that love should be uncomplicated, is beginning to feel irritation with Emma's sentimental effusions:

This so very experienced man did not distinguish the dissemblance of sentiments beneath the parity of expressions. Because venal or libertine lips had murmured similar phrases to him, he had only doubtful confidence in the candor of these. It was necessary to discount, he thought, exaggerated speeches masking mediocre affections; as if the fullness of the soul did not overflow sometimes in the emptiest metaphors, since no one, ever, can give the exact measure of his needs, or his conceptions, or his sorrows, and since human speech is like a cracked cauldron on which we beat out tunes for dancing bears, when we would like to draw tears from the stars. (*Madame Bovary*, 265)

This passage should be quoted more frequently when people talk about Flaubert's impersonality. It is interesting to note that Emma's tragedy stems in part from her inability to find words adequate to her feelings or her needs, and that the problem of expression is central, to her, as it was to her creator. More importantly, however, the paragraph is a statement of the insight that informs the whole novel: man in this world can never fulfill his needs or his conceptions; and life, like human speech, is a cracked and battered kettle on which men are condemned to try to produce sounds which will draw tears from the stars. *Madame Bovary* is a protest—not primarily against the Romantic conception of love (this has been too frequently overstated)—but against the very conditions of life.

This scene with Rodolphe is not the only one in the novel in which Emma's difficulties are compounded by the inadequacies of language. Early in her marriage, when she becomes aware that the "calm in which she was living was not the happiness of which she had dreamed. . . . she would have liked to confide in someone about these things. But how to give word to an elusive malaise, which changes its aspect like the clouds, which eddies like the wind? She lacked the words, the opportunity, the boldness." (55; 57)

There is also the tragic scene with Father Bournisien. One soft spring evening, after Emma has fallen in love with Léon, the ringing of the Angelus brings to her memory the convent chapel and the little girl she had been. Almost without realizing it, she goes to the church and seeks out the priest, "ready for any act of devotion, provided that she can absorb her soul in it." But speaking to the earthy, unkempt clergyman, whose attention is on the urchins who are arriving for instruction in catechism and who are roughhousing in the chancel, she is unable to formulate her need or her suffering. "Excuse me, Madame Bovary," says the pastor to this lost lamb who cannot articulate her distress, "but duty above all, you know. I have got to take care of my rascals." (159)

But power of expression, in the narrow and literal sense of this term, is not what Emma is primarily seeking. She longs for a self-fulfillment which she expects to find in a conventional and confused conception of romantic love and luxurious surroundings:

She confused, in her longing, sensuous luxury with the joys of the heart; elegant living and delicate feeling. Didn't love, like Indian plants, require cultivated soil and special temperature? Sighs in the moon-

light, long embraces, tears which bathe surrendering hands—all the
fevers of the flesh and the languors of sentiment were thus inseparable
from the balconies of great chateaux where leisure is abundant, from
a boudoir, curtained in silk, thick carpeted, from flowering planters,
from a bed on a dais, from the sparkle of precious stones, from orna-
mental liveries. (82)

   In a chapter astounding for its virtuosity, resonance, and
beauty, the author analyzes the sensations, impressions, experiences, and readings out of which this dream was created. Because,
in these passages, Flaubert is more successful in maintaining his
distance and his objectivity, and because his ever-present irony is
constantly pointing up the irrelevancy of the dream to the life
Emma must experience, informed and competent critics have in-
terpreted the novel as an indictment of Romanticism, or even of
reading. I must disagree. It is too easy, as Alfred Kazin has remarked in a quite different context, and perhaps too complacent,
to assume that Flaubert was angry only with his own century. He
was protesting, not the conventional opinions of his own time, but
the eternal conditions of life. Emma's tragedy would have been
the same had she never read *Paul et Virginie;* had she never seen
the blue porcelain plates whose legends "cut here and there by the
scratches of knives, glorified religion, the delicacies of the heart,
and the pomps of the court"; and had Walter Scott never made
her long to "live in an old manor, like those long-waisted châte-
laines, who, under the trefoil of the gothic arch, spend their days,
their elbows on the stone and their chins in their hands, watching
a white plumed knight ride in from the horizon, galloping on a
black horse." Her dream might have taken another form, but life
would still have made sport of her conceptions and her demands.

6.

*"Il fait une clientèle d'enfer; l'autorité le ménage et l'opinion publique
le protège."*

   The novel's subtitle, *Provincial Manners,* defines the atmosphere and the environment in which Emma is called upon to live.
The blue waters and warm skies, the picturesque mountains, and
the quaint costumes which she imagines must be replaced by the

sleepy, nondescript Norman village: "Here we are where Normandy, Picardy, and Ile de France come together, a bastard region where language is without accent and the landscape without character. Here they make the worst Neufchâtel cheese in the whole area; what is more, farming requires an investment, because it takes lots of manure to fertilize the friable, sandy, stoney soil." (96) In this uninspiring, dreary background, Emma's hapless and mediocre husband is perfectly at home:

Charles' conversation was as flat as a side-walk where the ideas of the man on the street passed in their everyday costumes, without exciting emotion, laughter, or dreams. He had never been curious, he said, when he lived at Rouen, to go see the Parisian companies that appeared at the theater. He could neither swim, fence, or fire a pistol and was not able, one day, to explain a riding term which she ran across in a novel. . . . One could learn nothing from this fellow, he knew nothing, desired nothing. He thought that she was happy; she resented his settled calm, his serene dullness, and the very happiness that she brought him. (57)

The boots he wears, the knife he carries, his lips trembling in the cold—seen, as we see them, through Emma's eyes—become symbols of his vulgarity and ineptitude. She will not be much more fortunate in the lovers she accepts: the coarse, cynical Rodolphe; the weak-willed, conventional Léon.

The inhabitants of Yonville l'Abbaye, as pictured by Flaubert, are a dull, depressing lot. Some of them, for example Lheureux, the dry goods merchant and money lender, whose usurous transactions bring about Emma's downfall, are also very black. But the supreme representative of provincial society, the ultimate incarnation of the bourgeois pomposity and mediocrity that the author so despised, is the self-important pharmacist, the ineffable Monsieur Homais—one of Flaubert's great creations. His speeches—and he cannot open his mouth without delivering an oration—are a long succession of stereotyped rhetoric, mixed metaphor, and pedantic vocabulary: "Why these festoons, these flowers, these garlands? Where was that crowd hurrying, like the waves of a furious sea, under the torrential rays of a tropical sun which poured its heat over our furrows?" (212) It is only fair to add that this is Homais' literary rather than his conversational style.

Among other things, Homais is a journalist and correspondent in Yonville for the *Fanal de Rouen*. A busybody, prying into everyone's affairs, he believes in progress, and prides himself on being an anticlerical and a Voltairian. As an apothecary, he is a professional man who has acquired the little learning which, we are told, is a dangerous thing. It is he, who, out of a desire to bask in reflected glory, constrains Charles to undertake the catastrophic operation on Hyppolite's clubfoot. Homais is always prepared to settle the problems of the world, and the triviality of his ideas is matched only by the pretentiousness of his speech. Squarely set in this world, his complacent stupidity makes him a force which nothing can resist. Physicians cannot make a living in Yonville because of the competition of his illegal, but anodyne, consultations. In the closing sentence of the novel, he is awarded the cross of the Legion of Honor.

The fact that the portrait borders on caricature does not make Monsieur Homais a less monumental creation. There is sufficient perspective and shading to make the figure terrifying in its dreadful reality. Homais flourishes, prospers, and basks in the same flat and dismal atmosphere that stifles all that Emma yearns for. He never suspects the shabby mediocrity of himself and his surroundings. He never dreams that men and women have other aspirations. He is the very symbol and incarnation of all that is most discouraging in the petty complacency of human stupidity.

Efforts, not very convincing, have been made to find real life models for Monsieur Homais. But the pharmacist, like the other characters in the novel, is much more than the portrait of a particular individual. He is the child of Flaubert's lifelong obsession with what he called the "bourgeois." Since the author intended no Marxist connotations when he used this word, we might better translate it as the "philistine" (it is true that he found the bourgeois society from which he had sprung composed primarily of philistines). Flaubert is repelled, yet at the same time, fascinated by the figure, by the mentality that reduces everything to stereotyped absurdity and platitude. When still not much more than an adolescent, he imagined a being named "le Garçon," who played an almost real role in his life and in the lives of his companions, the Le Poittevins and Chevalier. The Garçon seems to have been given sometimes to cliché, and sometimes to the caricature and ridicule of cliché. In later years, when Flaubert and his friends recalled their youth, the laughter of the Garçon was a recurrent memory. An important part of Monsieur Homais derives from this invention.

Many of Homais' speeches, like many other parts of the novel, are also drawn from the *Dictionnaire d'Idées reçues,* the *Dictionary of Accepted Ideas.* Flaubert conceived of this work while he was travelling in the Middle East; before he returned to Croisset, he had already jotted a number of entries, and he continued to add to it throughout his life. The *Dictionary* lists "in alphabetical order, on all possible subjects, what one must say in society to be a proper and acceptable man." (*Corr.,* III, 67) It is a compendium of the stereotypes and clichés which make up so much of human discourse. "Once one has read it, one must no longer dare to speak, for fear of saying naturally one of the sentences in it." (*Ibid.*) At the time of the composition of *Madame Bovary,* Flaubert was excited about the possibility of writing a preface to this work (he never did so): "I would attack everything. It would be the historical glorification of everything people approve. I would demonstrate that the majorities have always been right, the minorities wrong. I would sacrifice the great men to all the fools, the martyrs to all the executioners. . . . I would establish that, since it is within the reach of everyone, mediocrity alone is legitimate, and any sort of originality is to be spurned as dangerous, stupid, etc." (*Corr.,* III, 66) The preface was to have been written in such a way that the reader could not be sure whether his leg was being pulled or not.

As I have said, many of Homais' magnificent pronouncements are drawn from this compendium. It is because of Yonville and Monsieur Homais that *Madame Bovary* becomes a part of one of the three great themes or subjects to which Flaubert devoted his career: the theme of human stupidity (the two others are, of course, the sentimental education and the St. Anthony). From the *Leçon d'histoire naturelle,* written when he was a schoolboy, to *Madame Bovary,* and from *Madame Bovary,* through parts of the *Education sentimentale* and *Un Cœur simple,* to the posthumous *Bouvard et Pécuchet* this theme possessed Flaubert; he spent a large part of his life seeking to find a conception adequate to express its immensity.

In *Madame Bovary,* a foil to the anticlerical and Voltairian Homais is provided by the parish priest. Father Bournisien serves the faith quite as inadequately as the apothecary serves science. He fails to recognize Emma's call for help in the scene to which I have already referred; he is unable to guide her mystic aspirations in the months that follow her illness. The character is sharply etched and amply developed. He is not cursed with the pharmacist's indefatigable loquacity, but in every other way Bournesien is the clerical counterpart of Homais. A scene of high comedy develops as these two keep the vigil, the night before the funeral, beside Emma's body. Alternately, they quarrel and doze throughout the night; each time that they waken, the man of the church sprinkles the room with holy water; the man of science pours a bit of chlorine on the floor. Early in the morning, overcome by hunger, they partake of food and drink, "giggling a little without knowing why, impelled by that vague gaiety which seizes one after periods of sadness; and at the last sip of brandy, the priest said to the pharmacist, putting his hand on his shoulder 'we'll get along yet.'" (460)

In this dreary environment, surrounded by these dismal people, fulfillment for Emma was difficult indeed.

7.

"D'où venait donc cette insuffisance de la vie?"

In her efforts to understand the nature of her predicament, Emma invokes frequently her past and contrasts the hopelessness of her present situation with the freedom and promise of her girlhood. Here too, she resembles her creator. Flaubert took grim pleasure in revisiting the phantoms of his youth and in cataloguing his lost enthusiasms and his vanished hopes. Emma, for example, at the moment when she realizes that her relationship with Rodolphe has lost its pristine charm, receives, along with the annual gift of the turkey, a letter from her father. This paragraph, the stylistic values of which would be lost in translation, follows:

Elle resta quelques minutes à tenir entre ses doigts ce gros papier. Les fautes d'orthographe s'y enlaçaient les unes dans les autres, et

Emma poursuivait la pensée douce qui caquetait tout au travers
comme une poule à demi cachée dans une haie d'épine. On avait sé-
ché l'écriture avec les cendres du foyer, car un peu de poussière grise
glissa de la lettre sur sa robe, et elle crut presque apercevoir son
père se courbant vers l'âtre pour saisir les pincettes. Comme il y avait
longtemps qu'elle n'était plus auprès de lui, sur l'escabeau, dans la
cheminée, quand elle faisait brûler le bout d'un bâton à la grande
flamme de joncs marins qui pétillaient. . . . Elle se rappela des soirs
d'été tout pleins de soleil. Les poulains hennissaient quand on passait,
et galopaient, galopaient. . . . Il y a avait sous sa fenêtre une ruche
à miel, et quelquefois les abeilles, tournoyant dans la lumière, frap-
paient contre les carreaux comme des balles d'or rebondissantes. Quel
bonheur dans ce temps-là! quelle liberté! quel espoir! quelle abondance
d'illusions! Il n'en restait plus maintenant. Elle en avait dépensé à
toutes les aventures de son âme, par toutes les conditions successives,
dans la virginité, dans le mariage et dans l'amour;—les perdant ainsi
continuellement le long de sa vie, comme un voyageur qui laisse quelque chose de sa richesse à toutes les auberges de la route.   (238)[2]

This prose is the kind that Flaubert liked to write: rhythmic,
sonorous, and rich in suggestion and allusion. The ashes reveal,
fifty years before Proust, the mechanism of involuntary memory.
The past, thus conjured up, unfolds its wealth and promise in a
series of precise, clearly defined images and sensations. The inevitable contrast with the present follows, and the murky formless-
ness of the heroine's distress is sharpened and focused by the
final simile. The whole is appropriate to the circumstances of the
novel. There is not a sensation that Emma could not have experienced. Yet how suggestive it is of Flaubert writing to his friends
about the dear, dead days.

So life destroys Emma's dream. But she has still to learn the full
bitterness of the truth. Through most of her disappointments, she
continues to consider herself an exceptional victim of outrageous
fortune; others are enjoying the bliss that is passing her by:

[Charles] might have been handsome, witty, distinguished, attractive,
as those whom her boarding school friends had married doubtless
were. What were they doing now? In the city, with the noise of the
streets, the buzzing of the theatres, and the lights of balls, they were
enjoying the existence in which the heart dilates and the senses open
up. But her life was cold as an attic whose window faces the north,

and boredom, a silent spider, kept spinning its web in the darkness, in all the corners of her heart. (62)

And elsewhere: "All that surrounded her immediately, the dreary countryside, the half-witted small town business people, the mediocrity of existence seemed to her an exception in the world—a fluke of luck by which she was caught, while beyond extended, as far as one could see, the immense land of felicities and passions." (82)

It is only at the end of the novel that Emma senses that perhaps she is not the plaything of an unjust quirk of chance. When the affair with Léon has grown old, she sits down one afternoon in Rouen on a bench in front of her convent school and compares her present disillusionment with the "ineffable sentiments of love" to which, as a school girl, she looked forward. Her meditation continues: "Whence came then this insufficiency of life, this instantaneous decay of the things on which she leaned? . . . Nothing moreover, was worth the effort of a search; everything lied. Each smile hid a yawn of boredom, each joy a curse, each pleasure its disgust, and the rarest kisses left on one's lips only an unrealisable desire for a higher delight." (392)

When Emma understands thus what Flaubert thought he had learned—that life in general is miserable, dreary, stupid, and mediocre—that she is not the victim of a private injustice, that she has simply shared the common lot, the story is complete and her suicide follows very shortly. Here, I take it, lies the peculiar adequacy and propriety of Emma as a symbol. The commonplace woman represents better than a tragic hero the truth Flaubert thought he had apprehended. The suffering of an Oedipus, a Hamlet, or a René may be the compensation of their very superiority: a punishment exacted by the gods for the hero's pride. "Not so," replies the world of Flaubert's creation, "it is simply the destiny of all who dream or aspire."

8.

"L'ironie, pourtant, me semble dominer la vie."

To tell this story, Flaubert produced a work of almost classic form and proportion. The novel is divided into three parts which could easily be called the beginning, the development, and the conclusion. Part I contains nine chapters and runs, in the Conard text, to ninety-four pages. The setting is Tostes; the story is of Emma's marriage and its failure. Part II (fifteen chapters, two hundred and twenty-three pages) relates the heroine's quest for fulfillment, first in the platonic love for Léon, then in her involvement with Rodolphe. The action develops in the somewhat larger town of Yonville. Disillusionment and hopelessness follow her abandonment by Rodolphe, but the performance of *Lucia* and the singing of Lagardy provide fresh fuel for her longings. Part III (eleven chapters, one hundred and sixty-two pages) is devoted to the account of Emma's degradation and destruction in the affair with Léon, in the tissue of lies in which she gets herself entangled, and in her irresponsible financial manipulations. A large part of this development takes place in the city of Rouen.

If it is true, as Thibaudet and others have pointed out, that her suicide is the consequence, not of her love, but of her bankruptcy, it is also true that the indifference of Rodolphe and Léon to her plight is the crowning disillusionment: "Madness was seizing her, she became frightened and succeeded in getting hold of herself, confusedly, it is true; for she did not remember the cause of her horrible predicament; that is the question of money. She was suffering only from her love, and felt her soul taking leave of her through this memory, as wounded men, in their agony, feel their life flowing out through their bleeding sore." (432) The financial crisis is the symbol of the other, and the unity of theme is intact.

To give expression to this tragedy, Flaubert discovered striking and original stylistic devices. In our discussion of the composition of the novel, we saw that Flaubert was concerned about creating trivial dialogue that was to be nonetheless well written. He solved this problem, in part, by the skillful use of what the French call *style libre indirect,* an expression that seems to have no English equivalent. This method consists in the elimination of conjunctions and in the manipulation of tenses and pronoun references in such a way as to avoid the heaviness of indirect discourse.

A woman who had imposed such sacrifices on herself could certainly permit herself some whimsies.   (173)

. . . .

They [the days] were going then to follow one another now in an always similar progression, countless, and bringing nothing. Other lives, however flat they were, had at least the chance of an event. An adventure sometimes brought infinite changes of fortune, and the decor varied. But, for her, nothing happened, God had wished it so. (87)

These passages permit us to follow the course of Emma's inner monologue. But the novelist can likewise use it to maintain his distance, to dissociate himself from his personage, and to point up the confusion and the ironies of the situation. Léon is waiting for Emma to arrive for their rendezvous in the cathedral:

She was going to come shortly, charming, uneasy, searching out behind her the glances that followed her,—and with her flounced dress, her gold lorgnon, her thin shoes, in all sorts of elegancies which he had never enjoyed, and in the ineffable seduction of virtue on the point of surrender. The church, like a gigantic boudoir, was disposed about her, the vaults curved down to receive in the shadow the confession of her love, the stained glass was ablaze to illuminate her face, and the censers were burning to welcome her like an angel amidst clouds of perfume.   (331)

It is thus, in the original at least, that Flaubert gave "to prose the rhythm of verse (while leaving it distinctly prose)," and wrote "of ordinary life as one writes history or epic (without denaturing the subject)." The invention of a style adequate to the theme as he conceived it was indeed "a very great and very original endeavor." (*Corr.*, III, 143) It is the function of style to impose its own order of poetry and beauty on the trivial adulteries of the commonplace woman and upon the dismal flatness of middle-class country life. The banal must be made to seem interesting (and still not be distorted).

The author accomplishes this feat in part by being a better observer than other men. Just as any one who is a trifle fastidious will endeavor to avoid the ready-made expressions so dear to Monsieur Homais, the artist eschews the conventional, ready-made impression or observation. Jean Pommier has remarked that in Egypt both Flaubert and Du Camp visited a cave where both of them saw bats. But Flaubert alone added this detail to his account: "When they go out through the entrance, you can see blue air through their thin, grey wings." [3] Flaubert's poetic universe is made up of such rare sensations, of details which would be missed by the ordinary observer but which await the enchanter's wand (I am still paraphrasing Monsieur Pommier) to unfold their power and to characterize, for the reader, a personage or a landscape.

Thus the most ordinary objects, though they remain distinctly what they are, take on symbolic overtones which reveal the artist's vision. Flaubert's realism is based, not on accumulation but on meaningful choice. Hence every object, every detail has its role and its significance in the story. We have already seen how the things that Charles touches—his boots, his knife, his barometer, and the phrenological head—reveal the ineptitude and incompetence of the unfortunate Bovary. On two occasions, Emma's shoes are likewise transmuted into something more than themselves. After the ball at la Vaubyessard, when the heroine is putting away her party clothes, she observes that the sole of her slippers had been yellowed by the wax of the dance floor. The text continues: "Her heart was like them: through this contact with luxury, something which would not disappear, had been rubbed into it." (78) And there is the scene in which the love-struck adolescent, Justin, cannot stay out of the Bovary kitchen; he is fascinated by the sight of Emma's apparel, which Félicité, the maid, is ironing. She mistakes his interest:

Félicité was irritated at seeing him hang constantly around her. She was six years older than he, and Théodore, Monsieur Guillamin's servant, was beginning to court her.

"Leave me alone," she said, moving her jar of starch. "Go shell the almonds; you are always poking around women. Better wait for that sort of thing, nasty little boy, till you get some beard on your chin."

"Now, don't be cross. I'm just going to do her shoes."

And from the doorsill, he would get Emma's shoes all caked in mud —the mud of her rendezvous—which fell away in powder under his fingers, and he would watch it float up softly in a ray of the sun. (261)

This confusion of cross purposes and this juxtaposition of incongruities are characteristic. Félicité does not suspect the nature of Justin's adoration, and she misinterprets the reason for his presence in the kitchen. The mud that clings to Emma's shoes, each time she goes to meet Rodolphe, rises in golden mist before the eyes of the youngster, whose adoration leaves them spotless.

Symbols, metaphors, and juxtapositions of this sort occur on every page. The normal and the banal take on reflections, sheens, and shades of poetic value, so that the portion of reality that the novelist is describing becomes, in Philip Spencer's phrase, "a microcosm of universal destinies."

These destinies are most often tragic, and beset by the ever present ironies of life. "If *Bovary* is worth anything," Flaubert wrote early in the period of composition, "the book will not be lacking in compassion. Irony, however, seems to me to dominate life." (*Corr.*, II, 407) Despite statements to the contrary and despite the insistence of many critics upon the author's inhuman refusal of all emotion, the compassion which Flaubert sought is present throughout the work. The author does not let himself go in pity; he generally maintains his distance; but he makes us feel and share in the suffering of his creation. We agonize with Emma, despite our impatience with her silly conceptions and her wrongheaded infatuations. As was the author's intention, Charles, despite our irritation with his inadequacies, makes us feel for all widowers, and for all husbands whose wives find them incompatible. The paragraph in which le père Rouault returns home after his daughter's marriage is as moving as any comparable bit in literature and does not distort the subject one iota. The portrait of Catherine Leroux, fifty years a servant on the same farm, is unforgettable. I could multiply illustrations. The book is not lacking in compassion; yet Flaubert's sense of the irony of existence dominates every word and every situation.

We sometimes feel, as in the death scene, where, as B. F. Bart has pointed out, the author seems to abandon the distance he has maintained and to move closer to the heroine, where certain expressions come dangerously close to the merely pathetic, where the voice of the blind beggar produces a crash and a discord that some readers find embarrassing, that Flaubert employs irony to control a compassion that threatens to dissolve in pity, and that the impression of constraint that sometimes results from a reading of *Madame Bovary* is the consequence of this tension.

This irony is not always corrosive and bitter. During Emma's convalescence from the illness that followed her abandonment by Rodolphe, the author lets us glimpse, among the guests in the sick room, Justin, of whom we have already spoken. Justin's unselfish devotion is to become the means of Emma's destruction when he lets her into the laboratory where she finds the arsenic. Now the sight of her in bed, with her black hair rolling on her shoulders, is frightening to the boy in its extraordinary splendor. The text continues: "Emma doubtless did not notice his silent eagerness, or his timidity. She did not suspect that love, which had disappeared from her life, was palpitating there, under that coarse cloth shirt, in that adolescent heart which had opened to the emanation of her beauty." (299) Emma did not notice, but other persons noticed—and failed to understand. Like Félicité, Monsieur Homais thought that Justin's constant presence in the Bovary residence meant that he had designs on the maid. Then, the night after the burial, while Rodolphe and Léon were sleeping peacefully, there was someone else who, at that hour, was not sleeping:

On the grave, between the pine trees, a child was weeping, on his knees, and his chest, broken by sobs, was gasping in the darkness, under the pressure of an immense regret, softer than the moon and more unfathomable than the night. The gate creaked suddenly. It was Lestiboudois; he was coming to get his spade, which he had forgotten earlier. He recognized Justin scaling the wall and knew then what to conclude about the malefactor who was stealing his potatoes. (469)

Justin's grief and Lestiboudois' potatoes—

9.

"La Bovary, c'est moi."

The statement "I am Emma Bovary" which Flaubert is said to have uttered in the course of a private conversation with the Rouen journalist, Amélie Bosquet, appears at first glance to be another of the striking but paradoxical outbursts to which our author was given. However, as the frequency with which critics quote and discuss the phrase suggests, these words afford a key to the meaning of the work. There is a very real sense in which they express what may be the ultimate truth about the genesis and conception of the novel. Despite the real-life models whom the author undoubtedly studied, despite Madame Delamare, Madame Pradier, and the rest, the vision that informs the novel springs from impassioned conviction which has its seat in the deepest sources of Flaubert's being.

It is not because it is possible to find in the novel transmutations of the novelist's personal experience—instructive and legitimate as these rapprochements may be. It is only partly because we can identify, with Jacques Suffel, attitudes and hatreds that Emma shares with her creator. Like Emma, Flaubert was bored; like Emma, he longed for blue skies and exotic shores, for a luxuriant and luxurious life made meaningful by a faithful, all-absorbing love. Like Emma, he felt horror for "the platitudes of marriage" and for the mediocrity and meanness of bourgeois existence.

More importantly, he thought he had learned, very young, that his longings were the stuff of dreams that had no substance in this world where the bourgeois, the philistine, is everywhere triumphant and where mediocrity and meanness are everywhere dominant. This knowledge Emma discovered only too late. But it is the poetry of disillusionment that gives significance and human meaning to the story of Emma Bovary. The awareness of the disparity between the dream and its realization is the direct reflection of the temperament of the author; and in this sense, indeed, *La Bovary, c'est moi.*

Are we to conclude, then, that the dream is at fault, or is it the world? The author does not answer. We are free, if we wish, to condemn Emma's frivolity, her silliness, her mendacity, her lack of a maternal feeling. The author does not do so (his lawyer's defense of the book as an eloquent parable of sin and retribution was surely a legal device and not an esthetic conviction). The only alternative open to Emma was conformity. Her pathetic efforts to resist seem only to degrade her, but would she have been a better person had she been able to accept life in the Yonville Flaubert pictures, with Charles and Bournisien, the vicious Lheureux and the shoddy Monsieur Homais, as all that humans

GUSTAVE FLAUBERT

may reasonably hope for or aspire to? Once again, the author does
not say.

But he felt and assimilated her anguish and her tragedy. He
found the bond of humanity uniting the vaporous wife of the
country doctor and the erudite artist in the study at Croisset. If he
was the Emma who yearned and sinned and suffered, he was also
the Justin who loved her, who gave her access to the poison, and
who wept at night on her grave.

CHAPTER 6

Carthage

1.

"J'éprouve le besoin de sortir du monde moderne."

THE success of *Madame Bovary* made a personage of Flaubert and marked the beginning of a new phase of his life. In the fall of 1856, with the manuscript of the novel all but complete, he had rented an apartment on the Boulevard du Temple. From this time forward, he spent several months each year in Paris, generally taking up his residence there in January and remaining until May or June. The greater part of the actual composition continued to be done during the summer and autumn months in the study at Croisset. The sojourns in Paris were devoted, most frequently, to research and documentation. And his social calendar, in the capital, was full.

He frequented in the world of letters during the late 1850's Gautier, the Goncourt brothers, Sainte-Beuve, Renan, Feydeau, Baudelaire; and he was likewise a regular figure at the receptions of such fashionable *demi-mondaines* as Jeanne de Tourbey, Madame Sabatier, and Suzanne Lagier. In the 1860's he developed friendships with Taine, Turgenev, and George Sand; attended the Magny dinners; became a member of the intimate coterie of Princess Mathilda; and was entertained by the Emperor both at the Tuileries and at Compiegne. For a part of almost every year between the publication of *Madame Bovary* and his death, he participated in the whirl of Parisian life. We tend sometimes, in our admiration for the solitary laborer at Croisset, to lose sight of the extent and the brilliance of Flaubert's social activities.

As we have already seen, on the completion of *Madame Bovary* in 1856, Flaubert had rewritten and reduced *La Tentation de*

Saint-Antoine. Fragments of this work were published by Gautier in the *Artiste* in December, 1856, and in January, 1857. The novelist planned, apparently, to bring out the *Tentation* in book form, but the prosecution of *Madame Bovary* made him fear possible clerical attacks on the new production. The manuscript of *Saint Anthony*, consequently, went back once again to the desk drawer. We do not know what it was that led Flaubert to his book about the war between Carthage and her mercenaries. The letters of February, 1857, show him at a complete loss as to what his next subject would be.

On March 18th, however, when he wrote to Mademoiselle Leroyer de Chantpie, his mind was made up: "I am busy now at an archeological project on one of the least known periods of antiquity, a labor which is a preparation for another. I am going to write a novel whose action will take place three centuries before Jesus Christ, for I feel the need to get out of the modern world, into which my pen has dipped too much, and the reproduction of which tires me as much as the sight of it disgusts me." (*Corr.*, IV, 164) He was reading and taking notes in the libraries from morning until evening, and at home late into the night. Elaborate and laborious documentation continued through the spring and into the summer. At the end of June, he believed that he would shortly have read everything that touched his subject, even indirectly. He began writing in August or September, and he worked on the first chapter until December. In October, he had found the definitive title, *Salammbô*.

The task to which Flaubert had set himself was fantastic. His ambition was to resurrect a city and a civilization which had been extinct for two thousand years; which had left no posterity, no tradition dear to modern man; and about which, as he said, very little was known. He hoped to present men and women of this dead civilization as they really were, to make them feel and speak as they had when they trod this earth, and at the same time make them alive and interesting to modern readers. He was not an archeologist, nor yet an ancient historian. But the reconstruction of this vanished civilization was to be as scientifically accurate as human effort could make it. Flaubert wanted to describe Carthage and the Carthaginians with the same concrete detail that he had employed for Yonville l'Abbaye and its inhabitants. He found his material both in ancient text and in modern scholarship. His principal source was the description, in Polybius' *General History*, of the revolt of the mercenary soldiers of Carthage after the first Punic War, and the defeat and destruction of the rebellious horde by Hamilcar Barca.

Throughout the composition of *Madame Bovary*, Flaubert had complained about the flatness and lack of elevation in the material; and he had longed for an ancient and epic subject in which he could give vent to his taste for the strange and the splendid, the monstrous and the exotic. Phoenician Africa seemed made to order, but the composition of the new work was to prove just as difficult, just as slow and laborious, and just as painful as the earlier one. He had worked on *Madame Bovary* for four years and five months; *Salammbô* occupied him from March, 1857, until April, 1862—for more than five years.

In January, 1858, in the midst of the second chapter, he decided that he could not proceed until he had visited and explored the site of Carthage. In April, he set out on a second trip to North Africa. The visit lasted less than two months and was concentrated on Tunis, Carthage, Utica, and the countryside around these cities. Flaubert enjoyed himself, felt that he had accomplished a great deal, and returned in excellent health. But he threw away all that he had written of the novel. Back at Croisset on June 20th, he informed Feydeau:

> *Carthage* must be completely rewritten, or rather written. I am tearing it all up. It was absurd, impossible, false.
>
> I believe that I am going to find the right tone. I am beginning to understand my characters and to be interested in them. That in itself is a lot. I don't know when I shall finish this colossal labor. Perhaps not for two or three years. (*Corr.*, IV, 266)

This estimate proved too optimistic. For three years and nine months more the novelist was chained to his terrible task. The Battle of Macar, the sacrifice to Moloch, and the carnage, starvation, and cannibalism of the Pass of the Ax would require all the concentration and all the rewriting that had made the Commices such an ordeal. Each scene led to new reading and research. The author experienced doubts and periods of depression: "I believe

GUSTAVE FLAUBERT

that my eyes are larger than my stomach. Reality is almost impossible in such a subject. . . . Despite everything, I continue, but gnawed by anxieties and doubts. I find consolation in the fact that I am undertaking something worthy of esteem. . . . On the other hand, it may be stupid." (*Corr.*, IV, 379) In December, 1859, he wrote Feydeau:

You have to be absolutely crazy to undertake such books. At each line, at each word, I overcome difficulties for which no one will thank me and people will be right not to thank me. For if my system is false, the work is a failure.

Sometimes, I feel exhausted and tired to the marrow of my bones, and I think of death with avidity, as an end to all this anguish. Then my spirits rise slowly. I am exalted again and I fall back again—ever thus.

When people read *Salammbô*, I hope they will not think of the author. Few will guess how sad he had to be to undertake to resuscitate Carthage.   (*Corr.*, IV, 348)

So the work went forward in alternating moods of depression and joy. The copied manuscript was ready in April, 1862. After elaborate negotiation (Flaubert was adamant, among other things, in refusing to permit illustrations), Lévy brought out the volume in November. Its reception was a second triumph for the author.

2.

"ainsi mourut la fille d'Hamilcar"

This epic poem, as Gautier called *Salammbô*, opens as the Mercenaries are celebrating the anniversary of a victory with a banquet in Hamilcar's gardens at Megara, a suburb of Carthage. The barbarians are in Carthage waiting for their wage, which the government is unwilling or unable to pay. The presence of this large horde of armed outsiders, suspicious, and awaiting their due, alarms the town. Flaubert insists upon the motley, heterogeneous character of the army, composed of Africans of all races, Greeks, Gauls, and Portuguese, who do not understand each other's languages:

[90]

They felt alone, despite their numbers; and the great city which slept beneath them, in the darkness, frightened them, with its heaps of stairways, its lofty, black houses, and its vague gods, even more ferocious than its people. In the distance, a few lights glided on the port, and there were lanterns in the temple of Khamon. They remembered Hamilcar. Where was he? Why had he abandoned them once the peace was concluded? His disagreements with the Council were doubtless only a trick to destroy them.   (*Salammbô*, 10)

The soldiers liberate a small group of Hamilcar's slaves; among these is the Greek, Spendius, who becomes a leader of the insurrection and a major personage in the novel. As the drunkenness progresses, the Mercenaries burn and pillage, shoot arrows at the lions in their pens, and mutilate the elephants. A group of them penetrates into a private garden, catches, cooks, and eats the Barca family's sacred fish who wear rings and jewels in their mouths. This sacrilege brings Hamilcar's daughter, Salammbô, out of the apartments which she inhabits on the upper story of the house. Followed by a company of eunuch priests of the goddess Tanit, she descends into the garden to lament, in an ancient Chaldean dialect which only the priests understand, the death of the fish—and to berate the Mercenaries:

Nobody knew her yet. They knew only that she lived a retired life composed of pious exercises. Soldiers had seen her at night, at the top of the palace, on her knees before the stars, with eddying smoke rising from lighted incense burners. It was the moon that had made her so pale, and something of the gods enveloped her like a subtle vapor. Her pupils seemed to look out beyond earthly space. She walked bowing her head, and held in her right hand a little ebony lyre.   (14)

She sounds the note of the knell of Carthage which her father will repeat in Chapter 7: "Ah, poor Carthage, lamentable town. You no longer have to defend you the strong men of other days, who went beyond the seas to build temples on the shores." (16)

Uncomprehending but fascinated, the soldiers listen to Salammbô's song. Two in particular, the Numidian chieftain, Narr'-Havas, and the Libyan, Matho, are entranced. The latter pushes closer to her. To reconcile herself and the army, she pours wine into a golden cup and gives it to him to drink. "In my land," says a

Gaul, whose speech the multilingual Spendius translates to Matho, "when a woman gives a soldier a drink, she is offering him her bed." (19) At these words Narr'Havas flings a javelin which pins Matho's arm to the table. In the disturbance which follows, Salammbô and Narr'Havas disappear. Matho, aided by Spendius, who, as a slave, knows the house and the grounds, spends the rest of the night trying unsuccessfully to find Salammbô. Spendius likewise points out to the soldier that Carthage is helpless before the mercenary horde and that her wealth is theirs for the taking. In one of the many remarkable descriptions in the book, dawn breaks over the city.

This somewhat detailed analysis of the first chapter is intended to give the reader an idea of the rich strangeness of this book. It is impossible to discuss the fourteen remaining chapters so thoroughly. We shall simply trace now the main lines of the action. The Mercenaries are persuaded to leave the city and to set up camp near Sicca. Matho is obsessed with his passion for Salammbô. Negotiations over the soldiers' pay break down; hostilities begin; the barbarians return and camp before the now closed city. We see Salammbô on her terrace at night, worshipping the moon, the goddess Tanit. She longs for something she cannot quite imagine or articulate. She summons the priest, Schahabarim, who has educated her—begs him to let her penetrate into the sanctuary of the goddess. She yearns to see the idol, and the magnificent cloak, the sacred veil upon which the destiny of Carthage depends, the *zaïmph*, the touch of which kills the profane. The priest rebukes her sacrilegious desire.

Spendius offers to lead Matho into the fortified and guarded city, but first exacts of him a promise of obedience. They breach the walls through the viaduct that carries water into Carthage. It is night. Spendius directs Matho into the temple of Tanit, where they strip the goddess of the holy veil, or *zaïmph*. Matho wraps himself in the cloak. Suddenly he exclaims:

"Suppose I went to her? I am no longer afraid of her beauty. What could she do to me? I am more than a man now. I could move through flames, I could walk on the sea. I am borne by a force. Salammbô, Salammbô, I am your master."

His voice thundered. It seemed to Spendius that he was taller—
and transfigured. (100)

Spendius cannot restrain him, and they go to Hamilcar's palace.
Matho succeeds in penetrating into Salammbô's bedroom. He
shows her the *zaïmph*, says that he has stolen it for her. She is
fascinated, hesitates a moment, but gets hold of herself and calls
for help. Her servants arrive; but, because no one can touch the
holy veil and live, Matho escapes. Crowds howl at him as he
walks through the city, but dare not approach the *zaïmph*. He
makes his way safely through a gate:

When he was outside he took the great *zaïmph* from around his
neck and raised it as high on his head as possible.
The cloth, caught in the sea breeze, gleamed in the sun with its
colors, its jewels, and the forms of its gods. Matho, wearing it thus,
crossed the whole plain to the soldiers' tents, and the people on the
walls watched the fortune of Carthage move away. (109)

Spendius had slunk unnoticed out of the city and back to camp.
The capture of the *zaïmph* is a disaster for the Carthaginians and
a triumph for the barbarians. Its possession makes Matho the un-
questioned chief of the mercenary horde, who now receives reen-
forcements from all the African nations subject to Carthage. Together, they win a victory at Sicca; and the fate of the republic
trembles in the balance. At this point, the suffete, Hamilcar Barca,
the father of Salammbô, returns home. Despite the hatred which
the other rulers of Carthage feel for him, he alone can hope to
save the city, and he is made commander-in-chief in the war
against the Mercenaries. He raises a new army and defeats the
enemy in the battle of Macar. He lacks the strength, however, to
follow up his victory, is surrounded by the numerically superior
barbarians, and his destruction seems certain.
At this point, Schahabarim, the high priest of Tanit—partly in
an effort to strengthen his own faith by proving the power of his
deity, partly out of a desire to dominate Salammbô, and partly out
of thirst for vengeance for his lost virility—urges the suffete's
daughter to save the city by making her way alone into Matho's
tent to recover the *zaïmph* and return it to the temple. After per-

forming a ritualistic dance and wrapping her body in the sacred python, Salammbô sets out, reaches the Mercenaries' camp, and is taken to Matho's tent. Here she gives herself to the barbarian leader (or does he give himself to her?). An alarm in the camp draws Matho out of the tent. "Then she examined the *zaïmph;* and when she had contemplated it at length, she was surprised not to feel the happiness she formerly imagined. She remained melancholy before her accomplished dream." (268) She wraps the *zaïmph* around her and makes her way through the lines to her father's camp. She arrives at the moment when Narr'Havas comes up with his men, announces to Hamilcar that he has changed sides and will henceforth serve Carthage. The treachery of the Numidians and the recovery of the *zaïmph* bring to Hamilcar enough strength to change the course of the war. He rewards Narr'Havas by promising him the hand of Salammbô.

Assisted by the forces of his new ally, Hamilcar now breaks through the barbarian lines and takes his army into the city. The Mercenaries lay siege to the town, bringing catapults and other murderous machinery which is described in elaborate detail. The city starves; and, when Spendius succeeds in breaking the aqua-duct, it endures the torture of thirst. In a harrowing and detailed scene, the citizens seek divine aid by sacrificing the sons of the well born to Moloch. Rain falls abundantly, saving the town.

Hamilcar now succeeds in getting his army out of the city by sea. He outmaneuvers the barbarians and traps the bulk of their force in the Pass of the Ax. Here they are destroyed amidst atrocious scenes of starvation, carnage, cannibalism, and putrification. Matho, with a smaller force, massacres Hanno's army; but Matho is in turn captured by Hamilcar and forced to run the gauntlet of the populace of Carthage, which slowly tears him to pieces. He dies under the eyes of Salammbô, who has just been married to Narr'Havas. But the bride suddenly falls back stricken: "Thus death came to the daughter of Hamilcar, because she had touched the cloak of Tanit."

3.

"combien il a fallu être triste pour entreprendre de ressusciter Carthage."

For the background, the political situation in general, the movement of the troops, and the final outcome, Flaubert followed Polybius very closely. Matho, Spendius, and of course Hamilcar, are historical personages. The *General History* states, likewise, that, in order to secure the loyalty of the Numidian chieftain, Narr'Havas, Hamilcar promised him the hand of his daughter. On this slenderest of historical threads, a part of the plot is constructed.

Lacking an ancient model for *Salammbô*, critics have suggested a number of modern originals. The efforts to find physical likeness between the daughter of Hamilcar and Madame Schlésinger, or Madame de Tourbey, are plausible. The incident of the woman glimpsed at Saint Paul's Outside the Walls at Rome in 1851 may likewise be relevant. Even more convincing is the association with the Carthaginian maiden of the courtesan Kutchiuk Hanam, whom Flaubert visited in Egypt and whose dance he described in detail in the *Notes de Voyage*. Flaubert had physical models for his heroine, but the story of the love of Matho and Salammbô and their two brief encounters amidst the clamors of war with its overtones of mysticism and mythology, as Tanit, the female principle, is overcome by the devouring Moloch, is the invention of the novelist's imagination.

Flaubert's reconstruction of Carthage and her civilization is strangely and repellently splendid (with characteristic perversity, he told the Goncourt brothers that he had chosen the city because it was the rottenest place in civilization). The ferocious gods; the avaricious populace; the mercantile supremacy of the city (Flaubert never lets us forget that this was a commercial people); the cruelty of manners; the exotic animals in the courts and gardens; the high, black houses rising in terraces toward the temples of the Acropolis, with the sea on one side and the desert on the other—all these provide colorful variety and unity of tone and impression.

Hugo von Hoffmanstal has said that if *Madame Bovary* offers "the wonderfully built-up catastrophe of a life," *Salammbô* reveals "the wonderfully built-up catastrophe of a city," [1] one reduced to hiring its heroes and depraved to the point of shortchanging them out of their wage. Hamilcar echoes the lament of Salammbô when he warns the Elders: "You will lose your ships, your farms, your chariots, your swinging beds, and your slaves who wipe your feet. Jackals will sleep in your palaces, plowshares will overturn your tombstones. Only the cry of the eagle will sound over the heap of ruins. Thou shalt fall, Carthage." (155) The Mercenaries will be conquered, but history fulfills Hamilcar's prophecy: Carthage will fall.

Nonetheless, the city reconstructed by Flaubert's erudition, imagination, and the magic of his prose is impressive. The description of the town, as Salammbô sees it from the height of her terrace by night, may serve as an example of the many magnificent word paintings that distinguish the book:

La lune se levait à ras des flots, et, sur la ville encore couverte de ténèbres, des points lumineux, des blancheurs brillaient: le timon d'un char dans une cour, quelque haillon de toile suspendu, l'angle d'un mur, un collier d'or à la poitrine d'un dieu. Les boules de verre sur les toits des temples rayonnaient, çà et là, comme de gros diamants. Mais de vagues ruines, des tas de terre noire, des jardins faisaient des masses plus sombres dans l'obscurité; et au bas de Malqua des filets de pêcheurs s'étendaient d'une maison à l'autre, comme de gigantesques chauves-souris déployant leurs ailes. On n'entendait plus le grincement des roues hydrauliques qui apportaient l'eau au dernier étage des palais; et au milieu des terrasses les chameaux reposaient tranquillement, couchés sur le ventre, à la manière des autruches. Les portiers dormaient dans les rues contre les seuils des maisons; l'ombre des colosses s'allongeait sur les places désertes; au loin quelquefois la fumée d'un sacrifice brûlant encore s'échappait par les tuiles de bronze, et la brise lourde apportait avec des parfums d'aromates les senteurs de la marine et l'exhalaison des murailles, chauffées par le soleil. Autour de Carthage les ondes immobiles resplendissaient, car la lune étalait sa lueur tout à la fois sur le golfe environné de montagnes et sur le lac de Tunis, où des phénicoptères parmi les bancs de sable formaient de longues lignes roses, tandis qu'au delà, sous les catacombes, la lagune salée miroitait comme un morceau d'argent. La voûte du ciel bleu s'enfonçait à l'horizon, d'un côté dans le poudroiement des plaines, de l'autre dans les brumes de la mer, et sur le sommet de Acropole les

cyprès pyramidaux bordant le temple d'Eschmoûn se balançaient et
faisaient un murmure, comme les flots réguliers qui battaient le long
du môle, au bas des remparts.   (55)[2]

It is perhaps regrettable that Flaubert did not provide us with a
map. It is difficult to follow the marching and countermarching as
the hordes move back and forth over the Tunisian countryside.
The battle scenes and the siege are the delight of the armchair
strategist. Flaubert marshals his hosts, maneuvers his elephants,
charges the enemy with the skill of a general. The descriptions of
siege equipment, the catapults and the battering rams, are worthy
of an engineer. The brutality of it all is appalling. Violence and
bloodshed, callous cruelty and fiendish torture, suffering, starvation, death, and putrification accumulate in every scene, on nearly
every page. Yet with all its horrors, *Salammbô* attains an epic
splendor.

Readers who, like Louis Bertrand and Christian Murciaux, have
lived in North Africa, are impressed by the extent to which the
novel captures and reveals that continent in its eternal nature and
aspect. It is not only the landscapes: sky, sea, desert, and mountain; it is even more the multiplicity and intermixture of races,
peoples, and tribes; of religion, language, and custom. The mercenary army is the perfect symbol of the heterogeneity:

All the faiths, like all the races, met in these armies of Barbarians,
and one considered the gods of others, for they were frightening too.
Many mixed foreign practices with their native religions. Even though
one did not worship the stars, certain constellations being ominous or
propitious, one made sacrifices to them; an unknown amulet, found by
chance in a moment of danger, became a divinity; or else it was a
name, just a name, which one repeated without even seeking to understand what it meant. But by dint of pillaging temples, of seeing quan-
tities of nations and slaughters, many ended up believing only in fate
and death; and each night they went to sleep with the placidity of
ferocious animals. Spendius would have spat on the images of Jupiter
Olympian; however, he feared to speak aloud in the darkness, and he
was careful, every day, to put on his right shoe first.   (125 f.)

And there is the frequently quoted passage in which the univer-
sality of death becomes manifest through the concrete particulari-
ties and peculiarities of the burial customs of the several tribes:

The Greeks, with points of the swords, dug graves. The Spartans, removing their red cloaks, wrapped the bodies in them; the Athenians laid them with their faces toward the rising sun; the Cantabrians buried them under heaps of stones; the Nasamonians doubled them up with oxhide thongs; the Garamantians took them to be buried on the beach, so that they might be eternally washed by the waves; the Latins regretted that they could not collect their ashes in urns; the Nomades longed for the heat of the sands in which bodies mummify, the Celts for three bare stones, under a rainy sky, on a bay dotted with islands. (280)

We can only admire Flaubert's erudition. We are also brought up before the common mortality which unites these men separated by birth, creed, tongue, and custom.

Africa nourished likewise the novelist's sense of the grotesque. The juxtaposition of squalor and splendor, of color and filth struck chords in his being which resounded with poetic melancholy: "and sometimes, on breasts crawling with vermin, there hung on a slender cord, a diamond which the Satrapes had sought for, an almost fabulous stone whose value would purchase an empire." (299)

Despite its very real qualities and beauties, and despite the enthusiasm it still arouses in a limited group of readers, *Salammbô* is probably Flaubert's least significant, successful publication. The author has not quite managed to put the breath of life into his gigantic reconstruction. We do not really believe in Matho and Salammbô; we are not really interested in the fate of Carthage. Perhaps the most pertinent criticism was made by Flaubert himself, when he wrote Sainte-Beuve: "The pedestal is too large for the statue. Now, as one never sins by *too much*, but by *not enough*, a hundred more pages relative to Salammbô alone would have been necessary." (*Corr.*, V, 269) Even so, we wonder whether she could have been made human.

The contemporary reception of the novel by the public can be considered, however, a second triumph. The book sold well. It was parodied on the stage and caricatured in the periodicals. Empress Eugénie was ecstatic; a Madame Rimsky-Korsakof, in the costume of the daughter of Hamilcar, was the sensation of a masked ball at the court.

Critical opinion was mixed, but those who were less than enthusiastic recognized the seriousness of the work and treated the author with respect. Sainte-Beuve, now in regular relations with Flaubert, published three highly critical articles. Many of his strictures appear well taken. But such lengthy attention from the dean of all critics was in itself a compliment. Flaubert wrote a long, more than courteous reply in which he answered Sainte-Beuve point by point. He was not so kind to the German archeologist, Froehner, who had challenged the authenticity of his reconstruction. Quoting text and document, volume and page, Flaubert succeeded, not only in establishing the soundness of his learning, but in making his critic appear ridiculous.

Sainte-Beuve published Flaubert's long and interesting letter, along with his articles in the appropriate volume of the *Nouveaux Lundis;* and he quoted the academician Lebrun as saying of Flaubert: "after all, he has come out of all this a bigger man than before." Perhaps the closing word should be given to Baudelaire, who wrote his publisher, Poulet-Malassis: "As for *Salammbô*, a great, great success. An edition of two thousand bought out in two days. . . . A great book, full of faults. . . . What Flaubert has done, he alone could have done. Much too much bric-a-brac, but many grandeurs: epic, historical, political, and even animal. Something astonishing is the gesticulation of all those beings." [3]

CHAPTER 7

Bereavement and Immolation

1.

"Suis-je vieux, mon Dieu, suis-je vieux."

BECAUSE the order adopted in treating the several novels is logical (I hope) rather than chronological, it now appears necessary to jump from 1862 and the completion of *Salammbô* to 1875. The next two publications are the *Education sentimentale* of 1869 and the definitive *Tentation de Saint-Antoine* in 1874. I treated the latter in an early chapter because the condemnation of the manuscript of 1849 marked a most important milestone in the development of Flaubert. The *Education* is, in my opinion, his greatest accomplishment; I am anxious, therefore, to reserve my discussion of it to the last chapter so as to consider it in the conclusion of this study as the *summa* of the author's career. A quick glance at Flaubert's life in the years between the publication of *Salammbô* and the composition of the *Trois Contes* may now be helpful.

The study at Croisset is still the center of the picture and the creation of the work the important part of the tale. From 1864 until 1869, the composition of the *Education sentimentale* absorbed the great bulk of Flaubert's time and energy. From 1869 until 1872, except for the interruption occasioned by the Franco-Prussian war, he labored on the final version of the *Tentation*. He then began work on *Bouvard et Pécuchet*, which, with intermissions, occupied him until his death. These years saw also a good deal of frustrating activity in the field of the theater. In 1862-63, Flaubert, in collaboration with Bouilhet and the Count d'Osmoy, composed a dramatic fantasy of the type called a *féerie* in French. Despite Flaubert's efforts with the managers of theaters over a period of years, *Le Château des coeurs* was never to materialize on the stage. After Bouilhet's death, in 1869, he concerned himself with the production of his friend's play, *Mademoiselle Aïssé*, which, when at last presented in 1872, proved a total failure. The novelist also rewrote one of Bouilhet's old comedies, *Le Sèxe faible;* but he did not succeed in getting it performed. In March, 1874, his own political satire, *Le Candidat,* closed after four showings at the *Vaudeville,* thus admitting Flaubert to the *Société des auteurs sifflés.*

Life at Croisset changed. In April, 1864, Caroline Hamard married Ernest Commanville. The departure of his cherished niece and pupil took the last vestige of youth and gaiety from the house. Madame Flaubert, who was aging rapidly, was more and more difficult and withdrawn. She died in 1872, and the solitude and quiet of Croisset became absolute. The death of Louis Bouilhet in 1869 put an end to the weekends spent reading and working together. This bereavement marked a major break in Flaubert's life: "Why write, now that he is no longer here?"

In Paris, during the winter months, the novelist's social life continued. In 1866, he was awarded the cross of the Legion of Honor. But the circle of intimates kept shrinking. Between 1869 and 1873, one after the other, Sainte-Beuve, Jules Duplan, Jules de Goncourt, Maurice Schlésinger, Théophile Gautier ("he was the best of the group"), and Ernest Feydeau followed Bouilhet in death. Flaubert felt that he was becoming a fossil.

During the War of 1870, Prussian troops were quartered not only at Croisset (which they left wholly intact), but also in the Rouen apartment in which the author and his mother took refuge. The debacle left him humiliated and embittered. The cries of rage which the spectacle of the Commune drew from him and the hatred he expressed toward the rebellious workers are held against him to this day by such critics as Jean-Paul Sartre.

Despite bereavement and national catastrophe, however, Flaubert's work went on. Then a new blow struck. Ernest Commanville, his niece's husband, owned what had seemed to be a prosperous lumber business. He imported timber from Scandinavia and elsewhere, cut it in his own sawmill at Dieppe, and sold the lumber to French builders. In 1875, he found himself threatened with bankruptcy. Flaubert sold his farm at Deauville, which constituted the greater part of his capital, and turned the proceeds over to Commanville. The gesture was generous and absurd. The two hundred thousand francs were not nearly enough to save Commanville, whose business was liquidated. Flaubert, who had impoverished himself, was now to spend the rest of his life in serious financial difficulty and embarrassment. He was almost totally dependent on the Commanvilles, who were sometimes slow to forward the sums of five hundred or one hundred francs he needed to meet his obligations.

By February, 1875, two chapters of *Bouvard* had been completed. The author found it impossible to continue work amidst the domestic and financial anxieties occasioned by Commanville's difficulties. In September, after he had signed the deed that ruined him, he accepted the invitation of his friend, the biologist Georges Pouchet, to make a prolonged visit at Concarneau. He was impressed by, and envious of, the serenity with which Pouchet carried forward his research into marine life. The sight of the ocean brought him calm, and in October he announced his intention of beginning the *Légende de Saint-Julien,* to see whether he "was still capable of making a sentence."

When he left Concarneau in November, the work was well under way, and he completed it in his new apartment in Paris in January, 1876. The following month he began *Un Coeur simple,* which he concluded at Croisset in August. In February, 1877, *Hérodias* was ready; and Flaubert was in a position to publish a volume. These works are very short—compared to the novels, they are trifles—but the composition appears to have moved with an ease and rapidity unusual for the author. In March, the tales were published in two Parisian papers (Flaubert was happy to receive some money), and Charpentier brought out the volume in April. The author had the manuscript bound in morocco and presented it to his companion and neighbor, Edmond Laporte.

The latter was, along with George Sand and Maupassant, among the great friends of Flaubert's last years. The men lived close together, for Laporte occupied an estate a bit down the river from Croisset. The intimacy between the two grew warmer as the companions of Flaubert's youth disappeared. From 1870 forward, this new association, more than anything else, made the solitude of Croisset tolerable for the novelist. Laporte rendered favors and ran errands. It was he who cared for Flaubert when the latter broke his leg in the winter of 1879. The author constantly called on his friend for information he was seeking for his writing. L'Asiatique, as the novelist called him, carried out these bits of research cheerfully and efficiently, to the extent that one can say that he is intimately associated with the composition of both the *Trois Contes* and *Bouvard et Pécuchet*. He accompanied Flaubert on his trips of documentation for the last novel, and Lionel Trilling suggests that a part of their affection survives in the friendship of the two copyists. At the time of Commanville's first troubles, Laporte's endorsement of a note was a major factor in postponing the bankruptcy. The melancholy truth requires us to add that when, in 1879, he refused to commit himself farther in behalf of the lumber merchant, the beloved Caroline's bitterness was such that Flaubert had to stop seeing him. He had sacrificed his fortune to his niece's well-being; he was now compelled to deny a friendship that was dear to him. When Laporte came to Croisset to pay his respects after Flaubert's death, Madame Commanville had him ordered off the property.

2.

"je veux attendrir les âmes sensibles."

The *Trois Contes* offers an epitome of the several facets of Flaubert's genius. Each of the three stories is a little masterpiece. *Un Coeur simple* suggests the author of *Madame Bovary* and of the *Education sentimentale*. The *Légende de Saint-Julien l'Hospitalier*, with its evocation of an idealized medieval society in which the supernatural and the mystic play a dominant role, is reminiscent of the *Saint Anthony*. *Hérodias* is an archeological reconstruction of Judeo-Roman society at the moment of the beginning of the ministry of Christ. Flaubert himself expressed uneasiness about its similarity to *Salammbô*. Each of the three tales provides the anthologist with more representative material than does a comparable number of pages of excerpts from the great novels. Each of them is inspired by the Normandy from which Flaubert had sprung. The cathedral at Rouen possessed a statue showing Salome dancing before Herod, while the executioner prepares to decapitate the Baptist. Saint-Julien is found not only in a stained glass window in the same cathedral, but likewise in a statue in the church at Caudebec, which Flaubert visited with Du Camp in 1846. *Un Coeur simple* is composed of Flaubert's intimate memories of the country around Pont-l'Evêque, Honfleur, and Trouville. Each of the three tales tells the story of an immolation and a sacrifice; thus the book reflects the bitter experience of Flaubert's last years.

The heroine of *Un Coeur simple* is a servant, who has never been anything but a servant. Félicité's life is one long act of simple piety and selfless devotion. When, at the age of eighteen, she is jilted by the boy who has asked her to marry him, she leaves the farm where she is employed, goes to Pont l'Evêque, where a woman she questions in front of the inn hires her as maid. Then

For nearly fifty years, the housewives of Pont l'Evêque envied Madame Aubain because of her servant Félicité.

For one hundred francs a year, she did the cooking and the housework, sewed, washed, ironed, knew how to bridle a horse, fatten poultry, churn butter, and remained faithful to her mistress,—who incidentally was not an agreeable person. (*Trois Contes*, 3)

Aside from these years of competent and unceasing domestic labor, the story of Félicité's life is not much more than the account of the successive disappearances of the persons she loved and served. First of all, there are the children of her mistress who have the literary names of Paul and Virginia. Paul goes off to school and never lives at home again. Félicité focuses all of her great capacity for devotion on little Virginia. She, too, leaves for boarding school, where she eventually dies of tuberculosis. Félicité now pours her affection on her nephew Victor. His parents are obviously exploiting her; in due course, the boy goes to sea and dies of yellow fever in Havana. Félicité undertakes to comfort Madame Aubain; over the years she likewise ministers to a Polish refugee and to a cancer stricken indigent. The former moves away; the latter dies. A government official, who has lived in South America, presents her with a parrot. For years this bird receives her love and attention. When Loulou dies, she has him mounted and puts him in her room among her treasures—the shell work box that

Victor had given her; the toys, books, and clothing that had belonged to Virginia.

The years pass. She becomes deaf. Madame Aubain dies. Paul and his wife return to claim the furniture, but, as the house does not sell, Félicité lives on for years in the dismantled building. Nearly blind, she is now saying her prayers to the moulding parrot, which she associates with the Holy Spirit. In her last illness, she offers the parrot as an ornament for a street altar for the feast of the Corpus Christi. When the procession stops beneath her window, her agony has begun. The censers swing:

A bluish vapor rose into Félicité's room. She advanced her nostrils, breathing it in with a mystic sensuality; then closed her lids. The movements of her heart became slower and slower, weaker each time and softer, as a fountain stops playing, as an echo disappears; and when she exhaled her last breath, she thought she saw, in the opening heaven, a gigantic parrot floating above her head.   (63)

As Flaubert wrote Madame Roger de Genettes, "it is in no way ironic, as you may suppose, but on the contrary very serious and very sad. I wish to move people to pity, to draw tears from sensitive souls, being one myself. Alas, yes, last Saturday at the burial of George Sand, I burst into sobs on embracing little Aurore, and then on seeing the casket of my old friend." (*Corr.*, VII, 307)

The death of Sand on June 8, 1876, was another great loss and bereavement for Flaubert. This friendship dated from 1862 when Sand had published a perceptive criticism of *Salammbô*. Despite all the things that appeared to separate them, they found themselves united almost immediately by bonds of sympathy and affection. A recent biographer of the "good lady of Nohant" says that Flaubert was the friend of her old age; in the years that preceded her death, there was no one whom he regarded with more affection and respect. Their correspondence is one of the great esthetic dialogues of the century and a testimony to the breadth of their views and the greatness of their souls. He addressed her as *chère maître* and was in turn her *vieux troubadour*. He accepted her maternal admonishments as, in the serenity she had achieved in the last years of her life of stormy passions, she endeavored to soften his bitterness and to bring him to a kindlier view of his contemporaries and to a more human conception of literature and art. Flaubert defended himself and his attitudes. The letters he wrote her constitute the most striking expression we have of the convictions of his maturity. He was none the less shaken by her arguments, and the tenderness that suffuses *Un Coeur simple* is in considerable part a result of this influence. More than a year after her death, he wrote her son Maurice:

> You speak of your dear and illustrious mother. Except for you, I do not believe that anyone can think of her more than I. How I miss her. How I need her.
>
> I had begun *Un Coeur simple* with her alone in mind and exclusively to please her. She died when I was in the middle of my work. So it is with all our dreams.   (*Corr.*, VIII, 64)

Much of the story is composed of Flaubert's earliest memories of Pont l'Evêque, Trouville, and the surrounding country. Gérard-Gailly says that the house, *"revêtue d'ardoises,"* was still standing in the 1930's. It had belonged to the novelist's cousin or great-aunt, Madame Allais, who, according to the same scholar, was the original for Madame Aubain; despite the fact that he offers no evidence to support the last contention, most commentators have repeated his statement. Surely, however, we are likewise justified in seeing in Madame Aubain and in Félicité Madame Flaubert, grieving over the loss of her husband and daughter, and the Julie who served her for so many years. The farms, Toucques and Gefosses, belonged, by those names, to the novelist's mother (many other proper names are equally authentic). Gustave and Caroline Flaubert had doubtless skipped stones in the pond and fed the rabbits, as Paul and Virginia do on their visits to the farms. As a boy, the novelist had stayed at the inn of the Agneau d'or and had known la mère David over many a summer at the Trouville beach. The parrot may even be one of the memories of these vacations. Félicité, almost run down by a stagecoach, falls into a ditch at exactly the spot where Flaubert suffered his earliest seizure. In April, 1876, just before he began the story, the author revisited the area to refresh his impressions and indulged in a "bain de souvenirs. Am I old. Dear Lord, am I old."

It is likewise permissible to see, along with Mr. Trilling, something of Flaubert in Félicité herself. Like her, he was devoted to his niece; like her, he was exploited by his relatives; like her, he was living alone in a dead and abandoned house; like her, he filled his study with sentimental souvenirs and objects that had belonged to the beloved departed.

Perhaps the best example of Félicité's selflessness, of the fact that her real existence was that of the people to whom she was devoted, is found in the paragraphs describing Virginia's first communion and the classes in catechism that preceded it. The servant's religious education had been neglected. It was at these classes that she heard for the first time the great Bible stories. The Old Testament inspired respect for the Most High and fear of his wrath. She wept over the Passion:

Sowing, harvest, wine presses, all these familiar things of which the Gospels speak, were in her life; the passage of God had sanctified them; and she loved lambs more tenderly for love of the Lamb, doves because of the Holy Spirit.

She had difficulty imagining his person; for he was not only a bird, but also a fire, and at other times a wind. It is perhaps his light which flutters at night at the edge of swamps, his breath which pushes the clouds, his voice which makes bells harmonious; and she stayed in worship, enjoying the coolness of the walls and the quiet of the church. (*Trois Contes*, 24)

So Flaubert prepares the confusion between the parrot and the Holy Ghost at the end of the tale. Félicité participates in Virginia's religious life, imitates her observances, fasts, and confesses with her.

The day of the first communion comes. Throughout the mass, Félicité is in anguish. After the triumphant chant of the *Agnus Dei*, the boys and girls go forward to receive the host:

When it was Virginia's turn, Félicité leaned forward to see, and with the imagination given by real tenderness, it seemed to her that she was herself that child, her face became hers, her dress clothed her, her heart was beating in her breast; at the moment when she opened her mouth while closing her lids, she almost fainted away.

The next day early, she presented herself in the sacristy so that the priest might administer the communion to her. She received it devoutly, but did not experience the same rapture. (25)

It is not only that Virginia's experience is more significant to Félicité than her own. We are also confronted by the author's constant insistence upon the failure of reality to live up to the promise of the imagination.

Anthony Thorlby calls *Un Coeur simple* "Flaubert's undisputed masterpiece" (there is, of course, no lack of readers prepared to dispute the contention). However that may be, the tale is very great. In its exemplary sobriety, *Un Coeur* contrasts sharply with the color and drama of the story which follows. The *Légende de Saint-Julien l'Hospitalier* reflects the splendor of the stained glass window which inspired it. Julien grows up in an idealized, patriarchal, medieval manor. He learns early to hunt; and, as the years pass, the senseless orgiastic slaughter of animals becomes an obsession and a mental aberration. On a fantastic and hallucinating day of hunting with dogs and falcons of several breeds and with an armory of exotic weapons, he kills animals and birds the mere catalogue of whose names would run more than a page. At the end of it all, a prodigious stag with an arrow in his head approaches and repeats three times "Cursed, cursed, cursed. Some day, ferocious heart, you will assassinate your father and mother." (93)

Horrified by this prophecy, Julien leaves home in an effort to make its fulfillment impossible. He becomes a soldier of fortune, does mighty deeds, defends the right, wins great fame, and finally marries the daughter of the emperor. He retires to a magnificent palace; but, believing that the stag's curse is still upon him and that the death of his parents is bound up with the killing of animals, he refuses to hunt. Then one night he yields to the temptation, and finds himself surrounded by mocking beasts against which his weapons are powerless. Meanwhile his parents, who have been seeking him for years, appear at his palace. His wife welcomes them, gives them her own bedroom, and goes to another apartment. Julien returns home from his fantastically frustrating hunt. In the semi-darkness, he perceives a man and a woman in his wife's bed, thinks he has been deceived, and kills them both. He sets out alone as a mendicant hermit, establishes himself on the bank of a river as a ferry-man. One stormy night, he brings a horrible leper across the stream, feeds him in his hut, warms him in his bed. The leper grows large and radiant, the heavens open, and Jesus Christ carries Julien to paradise.

The story is found in the *Golden Legend*, but Flaubert's source was apparently a nineteenth-century account of the stained glass in the Rouen cathedral. According to Du Camp, Flaubert considered making a book from the legend as early as 1846 when he saw a statue of St. Julien in the church at Caudebec. He took notes on venery during a vacation with Laporte in Switzerland in 1874; and he began composition, as we have seen, after the sale of his property in 1875.

As Taine pointed out, the legend in stained glass provides the tone and color. The Middle Ages are thus idealized; it is medieval society as that society dreamed of itself; a patriarchal and chivalrous world in which the supernatural is matter of course. The initial account of life in the manor of Julien's birth is a classic description of idealized medieval domesticity. The hunting scene, with its strange enumeration of dogs, falcons, beasts, and weapons achieves a dreamlike, supernatural unreality: "But Julien did not grow tired of killing, turn by turn bending his crossbow, unsheathing his sword, thrusting with his cutlass, and thought of nothing, had no recollection of anything at all. He had been hunting in an unspecified country for an undetermined length of time, by the very fact of his own existence; everything being accomplished with the facility one experiences in dreams." (91)

In places, the *Légende de Saint-Julien* attains a magnificence and concision of expression rarely equalled elsewhere. Certain sentences, splendid in their simplicity, realize hauntingly powerful evocations:

Il connut la faim, la soif, les fièvres et la vermine. Il s'accoutuma au fracas des mêlées, à l'aspect des moribonds. Le vent tanna sa peau. Ses membres se durcirent par le contact des armures; et comme il était très fort, courageux, tempérant, avisé, il obtint sans peine le commandement d'une compagnie. (97)

. . . .

Des esclaves en fuite, des manants révoltés, des bâtards sans fortune, toutes sortes d'intrépides affluèrent sous son drapeau, et il se composa une armée.

Elle grossit. Il devint fameux. On le recherchait. (98)

Il s'en alla, mendiant sa vie par le monde.

Il tendait sa main aux cavaliers sur les routes, avec des génuflections s'approchait des moissonneurs, ou restait immobile devant la barrière des cours; et son visage était si triste que jamais on ne lui refusait l'aumône. (115)[1]

Nowhere has Flaubert achieved greater stylistic mastery.

The third tale, *Hérodias*, tells the gospel story of Salome's dance and the decapitation of John the Baptist. The author stated his intention in a letter to Madame Roger des Genettes: "The story as I understand it has nothing to do with religion. What charms me here is the official mien of Herod (who was a real prefect) and the savage figure of Hérodias, a sort of Cleopatra and Maintenon. The question of races dominated everything." (*Corr.*, VII, 309)

As has already been suggested, we are in the mood of *Salammbô*, and the archeological reconstruction of the Judeo-Roman world is elaborate. A tympanium of the main portal of the Rouen cathedral contains a thirteenth-century sculptural group depicting the death of the Baptist. Salome appears standing on her hands in a pose that suggests the one with which her dance ends in the tale. For the other movements of her dance, the author drew on the memory of his visit in 1850 to the Egyptian courtesan, Kutchuik-Hanem, and on his travel diary. For the archeological and historical aspects of the story, he did the scrupulous research that accompanied all his writing.

Taine considered *Hérodias* the most successful of the tales. His letter congratulating the author of the *Trois Contes* is interesting enough to quote at length:

Each tale is a complete unit, learnedly balanced; one recognizes the master, the man who knows how to compose, to harmonize his effects, who does not permit a feature, not a word, that does not contribute to the final effect. What is more, your calm, your perpetual absence is all powerful. . . . In my opinion, the masterpiece is *Hérodias*. *Julien* is very true, but it is the world imagined by the Middle Ages, and not the Middle Ages themselves; just what you wanted, since you were trying to produce the effect of a stained glass window, that effect is there, the pursuit of Julien by the animals, the leper, all the purest ideal of the year 1200. But *Hérodias* is Judea in the year 30 A.D., the real Judea, and much more difficult to render, because it is a question of another race, of another civilization, of another climate. You are very right to say that at present history and the novel can no longer be distinguished.—Yes, on the condition that one writes novels as you do. These 80 pages tell me more about the surroundings, the origins, and the background of Christianity than the work of Renan; yet you know how much I admire his *Apostles,* his *Saint-Paul,* and his *Anti-Christ.* But the totality of manners, sentiments, and setting can be rendered only by your method and your lucidity. . . . It is as fine as, and lighter than, *Salammbô.* Nothing more profound than the intimate antagonism of the Jew and the Latin. That's all, my dear friend, I clasp your hand and congratulate you.[2]

This letter might well conclude a study of the *Trois Contes* were it not for the curious fact that Taine makes no mention of *Un Coeur simple.* To fill this lacuna we shall have recourse to an essay by Ford Madox Ford, taken from a chapter of a book with the title *Between Saint Dennis and Saint George.* The work, published in 1915 in the midst of World War I, can perhaps be classified as propaganda. The future of the world, in Ford's view, depended on the preservation of the values represented by French and British civilization. In the chapter entitled "Félicité," the author finds Madame Aubain and her servant the very symbols of the virtues that the Anglo-French troops were fighting to preserve. He urges us to read the description of Madame Aubain's *salle,* quotes it, then continues:

You will then know something of France, for France is *la salle de Madame Aubain,* where she sits day after day against the white wainscoting; there will be eight mahogany chairs, an old piano under a barometer; an arm-chair with a tapestry back will be on each side of the yellow marble mantelpiece, Louis Quinze in style. The clock in the center of the mantelpiece will represent a temple of Vesta, and all the room will smell a little of mould because the floor is a little lower than the garden. And when you have this picture well before you, you will find that there will rise in your mind the reasonably correlated idea that there must be thousands and thousands of such houses all over France from Alsace to the mouth of the Rhone—thousands and thousands of tranquil, useful households, where there is a touch of style in the tapestried arm-chairs, the yellow marble mantelpiece,

Louis Quinze in tradition, the clock and barometer—where, in fact life is quite decorous, sober, and more tenacious than the life of any other country in the world. Out of such small material indeed, and managing life with such frugality, these people achieve an existence of dignity and common sense. And that should be a great lesson to us.[3]

For Taine, *Hérodias* explains the Judeo-Roman world and the origin and background of Christianity. For Ford, *Un Coeur simple* is the perfect expression of the virtues that make contemporary France great. The little masterpieces that compose the *Trois Contes* are striking examples of the several facets of Flaubert's genius.

CHAPTER 8

Copy and Culture

1.

"J'en ai gros sur le coeur."

IN June 1877, with the *Trois Contes* published and successful, Flaubert returned to the manuscript of *Bouvard et Pécuchet* (we have seen that he had completed two chapters of this novel in 1874–75). This work was to occupy him until his sudden death in 1880, at which time he had not quite brought it to completion. These last years were saddened by financial distress and embarrassment. "My heart is heavy," he wrote Léonie Brainne in December, 1878:

and it is not the lack of money, the privations which are its consequence, and the complete absence of liberty to which I am constrained, no, it is not all that which makes me rage. But I feel soiled in my mind by these low preoccupations, by these commercial dialogues. It seems to me that I am becoming a grocer. Imagine an honest woman forced to prostitution in a brothel, some one with habits of cleanliness rolled in a street-cleaner's cart, that is my situation.

(Corr., Supplément, IV, 136)

In 1879 and again in 1880 he had to forego his winter residence in Paris. As he wrote Maupassant in January, 1879, "If I do not go to Paris, it is because I haven't a penny. That's the whole mystery, and because I have no lodging either having turned mine over to my niece, until her husband's business is definitely settled—and we know what's going to become of us and what he will do." [1] Legal summons to meet creditors' demands poured into Croisset right up to the eve of Flaubert's death. The novelist appears to have signed any papers that the Commanvilles presented, and to have understood very little of what was going on: "I was completely unaware that I had borrowed 50,000 francs." (*Corr.*, Supplément, IV, 323)

The solitude at Croisset was broken only rarely by visits from the Commanvilles and from Paris friends, and even more rarely by social engagements in Rouen where he had formed affectionate ties with Charles Lapierre and the "three angels," as he called Madame Lapierre, her sister Madame Brainne, and her friend, the actress Madame Pasca. On January 25, 1880, he wrote: "I have spent two and a half months absolutely alone, like the bear of the caverns, and all told, perfectly happily, despite the fact that I see no one; I did not hear stupid things said. The inability to bear human stupidity has become a disease with me, and the word is weak. Almost all humans have the gift of exasperating me, and I breathe freely only in the desert." (*Corr.*, VIII, 356)

After May, 1878, he made only short stays in Paris. Here he saw old friends—Taine, Renan, Turgenev, Jules de Goncourt; and he was admired and venerated by the new generation of novelists —Zola, Daudet, Huysmans, Paul Alexis, and especially by Guy de Maupassant, the nephew of Alfred Le Poittevin. In an effort to relieve Flaubert's financial distress, these friends initiated a campaign to have him appointed librarian at the Mazarine. They acted, however, with such indiscretion that the novelist's poverty became a subject of conversation in the salons. When *Figaro* printed a front-page article detailing his financial difficulties and excoriating the indifference of the authorities to his plight, Flaubert, immobilized at Croisset by a broken leg, felt stifled by shame and rage. The appointment to the Mazarine went to his old friend, Frédéric Baudry; but in May, 1879, Minister of Education Jules Ferry nominated the reluctant, humiliated author to an honorary position carrying a stipend of three thousand francs a year—enough, but no more than enough, to spare him further privation. Despite his distaste for the whole situation, he was touched and comforted by the countless testimonies of friendship and admiration which poured in upon him during these trying months.

In September, 1879, Flaubert made what proved to be his last visit to Paris, then returned to face the lonely winter at Croisset. In January, he began the final chapter of *Bouvard et Pécuchet*. In

February, he read the proof of the short story "Boule de Suif,"
which his disciple Maupassant was to contribute to the *Soirées de
Médan* and he proclaimed the tale a masterpiece. At Easter, Zola,
Daudet, Goncourt, Maupassant, and Charpentier were guests at
Croisset. On April 24th, Lapierre and his other Rouen friends entertained him at dinner to celebrate the feast of St. Polycarp.
Flaubert, planning to go to Paris for a prolonged stay early in
May, was looking forward to seeing his friends in the capital. The
departure was set for May 9th. On May 8, 1880, with his suitcases
packed, he suffered a cerebral hemorrhage and died without re-
gaining consciousness. On May 11th, in the presence of a number
of prominent literary figures, the burial rite was said in the church
at Canteleu; and Gustave Flaubert was laid to rest beside his father, his mother, and his sister in the Monumental Cemetery at
Rouen.

A few months later, the not quite complete *Bouvard et
Pécuchet* appeared in *La Nouvelle Revue;* in March, 1881, it was
published as a volume by Lemerre.

2.

"copier comme autrefois."

Flaubert's posthumous, unfinished work is perhaps the one with
which critics have the most difficulty. Its meaning is hard to come
by. François-Denis-Bartholemée Bouvard and Juste-Romain-
Cyrille Pécuchet, names which the author worked out with care,
meet on a bench along the Canal St.-Martin in Paris on a hot,
summer afternoon. Both are copy clerks, and they soon discover
that they are drawn to each other by deep affinities of character
and taste. When Bouvard comes into an inheritance, Pécuchet
realizes his savings; and the two decide to retire to the country.
They purchase a farm at Chavignolles on the Norman plateau
between Falaise and Caen; and here, at the age of forty-seven,
they undertake to master all the sciences and disciplines of human
culture. They carry out their experiments in agriculture, landscape
architecture, preserving and distilling, chemistry, medicine, and
geology with a naïve, ingenuous, and frequently inept enthusiasm
which at worst leads to disaster and at best to frustration or bore-

dom. Their sheep die, their fruit trees fail to produce, their preserved meat spoils; and the cordial, which they invent and plan to market under the name Bouvarine, blows up in their faces as they attempt to distill the first batch. After the sciences, they study history, literature, philosophy, and religion. In each case the uncertainties, the obscurities, and the contradictory authorities leave them weary and confused. They adopt two brutalized, homeless orphans and begin an equally disastrous experiment in education. The manuscript breaks off here.

We know, however, from Flaubert's notes and from his letters that at the height of their discouragement, the two self-taught encyclopedists were to decide to "copy, as we did formerly," and to order a double writing desk on which they can work together. Authorities disagree as to which of Flaubert's several collections of absurdities they were to copy. It seems unlikely, however, that it was the *Dictionnaire des idées reçues*, on which the novelist had drawn heavily for this and other books, and which could not, it seems, have been available to the two clerks. It appears probable that they were to transcribe the so-called *Sottisier*, an incredible collection of absurdities and lapses that Flaubert had gleaned over the years in the work of the most illustrious writers. The manuscript of this compilation was found in the dossier of papers pertaining to the novel. It includes, for example, Chateaubriand's oft-quoted pronouncement on Napoleon: "He was a great winner of battles, but, aside from that, the poorest general was more able than he." So Bouvard and Pécuchet were to end their lives as they had spent them, with ink, erasing knives, and sandarac, copying extracts they had noted in their days of study and experiment. They were to compile an anthology of the errors and ineptitudes of which even the greatest minds are capable. It seems most unlikely that they were to hit upon these howlers inadvertently.

Like the concepts of *La Tentation de Saint-Antoine* and *L'Education sentimentale*, the idea of this novel occupied Flaubert all his life. It is customary to refer to the *Leçon d'histoire naturelle; genre commis*, a satirical sketch in the style of the then popular physiologies, which Flaubert composed at the age of fifteen as the earliest effort to develop the theme. The *Dictionnaire des idées reçues*, the creation of M. Homais, and certain characters and incidents of *L'Education sentimentale*, all attest to the novelist's preoccupation and fascination with human stupidity and pretension. He had seriously considered beginning *Bouvard* in 1863, but he had abandoned the idea in favor of the *Education sentimentale*. But ten years later, after the completion of the definitive *Tentation de Saint-Antoine*, the theme drew him again and held him, this time, until his death.

3.

"L'insupportabilité de la sottise humaine est devenue chez moi une maladie."

If *La Tentation de Saint-Antoine* is the poem of the helplessness of man before infinity, *Bouvard* was to be a satire of the stupidity of man on this earth. There is little doubt that Flaubert intended, at first, to make the book a violent attack upon the nineteenth-century bourgeois culture he so despised. "I shall vomit on my contemporaries," he wrote in 1872, "the disgust they inspire in me, were I to burst my chest while doing it. It will be broad and violent." (*Corr.*, VI, 425) It seems certain too that he first conceived of his two heroes as consummate examples of bourgeois mediocrity and imbecility. He thought of entitling the work "the two wood lice"; his irony, throughout the book, but particularly in the early chapters, points up the grotesque ineptitude of the two little men who spend their lives copying papers. In April, 1875, he wrote Madame Roger des Genettes: "Bouvard and Pécuchet occupy me to such a point that I have become they. Their stupidity is mine, and it is killing me. You have to be cursed to have the idea of such books." (*Corr.*, VII, 237)

But something happened as the novel developed. The dean of Flaubert scholars, René Dumesnil, pointed out many years ago that Bouvard and Pécuchet are not imbeciles. They are comic characters, if one wishes; they have their share of follies and foibles; the mental indigestion that results from their efforts to absorb, rapidly and without preparation, the accumulated knowledge of mankind is laughable; but in regard to their effort to live by the mind, Flaubert is plainly on their side. The first consequence of their friendship and association, while they are still in Paris, is the broadening of their minds:

They inquired about discoveries, read prospectuses, and as a result of that curiosity, their intelligence developed. At the end of a horizon each day more distant they perceived things at once confused and marvelous. . . .

And having more ideas, they had more sorrows. When a stage coach passed them on the street, they felt a need to depart with it. The flower market made them sigh for the countryside.

(*Bouvard et Pécuchet*, 12)

Despite the comedy of their discomfitures and failures, Bouvard and Pécuchet are able to learn; and their knowledge, unabsorbed and undigested though often it be, distinguishes them from the mediocrity of the people who surround them in Chavignolles. Because they are curious, because they ask questions, because they do not always accept popular opinion, they are generally despised in the village:

The evidence of their superiority gave offence. Since they defended immoral theses, they must surely be immoral; calumnies were invented. Then a pitiable faculty developed in their minds, that of seeing stupidity and of no longer tolerating it.

Insignificant things made them sad: advertisements in the newspapers, a smug profile, a silly reflection overheard by chance.

Thinking about what was said in their village, and about there existing as far as the antipodes, other Coulons, other Marescots, other Foureaus, they felt as though all the heaviness of the Earth were weighing down upon them.

They went out no more and entertained no one.   (292)

Here, the copy clerks have become close kin to the author for whom the inability to bear human stupidity had become a disease, and who found contentment in solitude because he was not irritated by inept remarks. Here too the novelist has plainly come out on the side of the two grotesque students and against the townspeople who find their opinions and activities ridiculous. Bouvard and Pécuchet are not imbeciles; neither are they the "wood lice" that Flaubert orginally planned they should be.

Wood lice, to paraphrase Mr. Trilling, are not capable of friendship. The two copy clerks are, and it is the depth and warmth of their affection and esteem for each other that give the book its human charm and much of its interest. The reader shares the delight and satisfaction they derive from their meals and from their walks together. They are alike in their naïve curiosities and enthusiasms, but they are sufficiently differentiated otherwise so that their encyclopedic reading and research become the basis for a genuine dialogue. Pécuchet, tall and thin, is perhaps the more serious; he is more confident, more optimistic about human destiny and man's ability to cope with his problems. Short, fat, and balding, Bouvard tends to cynicism. Thus their speculations and conversations, despite the many silly things they say, become meaningful exchange. One complements the other, with the result that at times they are capable of really profound observations.

Like his heroes, Flaubert had a genius for friendship and dialogue. He bound to him, by the closest of ties, the men and women he liked and admired. Let us recall the roles of Le Poittevin and Bouilhet and to a lesser extent Maxime Du Camp in his early life and work. His closeness to George Sand was a running debate—a constant discussion and exchange of frequently opposing views, clarified and animated by affection and sympathy. The intimate association with Edmond Laporte, however, is the one that is most pertinent to the discussion of *Bouvard et Pécuchet*.

Like the two clerks, Flaubert and his friend made together the trips for documentation that the book entailed. Like the clerks, they worked together on the encyclopedic readings and study that went into the novel. It was Laporte who discovered and copied the absurdities and infelicities of medical authors found in the *Sottisier* which was presumably to compose the second volume of the novel.

Flaubert's friends and peers in Paris—Zola, Taine, and Turgenev—were alarmed and dismayed at the prodigious amount of research and note taking in which the novelist engaged; and they urged him to make the work shorter and lighter. The author felt that the only way he could avoid pedantry in this effort to realize the "comedy of ideas," in this "pretension to make a review of all modern ideas," was to be inclusive: "This superabundance of notes permits me not to be a pedant; of that I am sure." (*Corr.*, VIII, 356) He claimed to have read in preparation for *Bouvard* fifteen hundred volumes that he would not otherwise have examined. The intentions of Flaubert and his research were no less encyclopedic than those of his personages.

Somehow, during the course of the composition of the novel, Bouvard and Pécuchet, while still remaining comic characters, not only ceased to be the idiots that Flaubert had originally imagined, but assumed a life of their own, which becomes a not unsympathetic caricature of the life of the master of Croisset. They read, amass notes, and pursue their chimeras with the same dogged persistence as he. Their friendship is a reflection and tribute to the bond that united their creator and Laporte. In the words of Albert Thibaudet: "Out of their nature as imbeciles, he [Flaubert] brings a critical nature, like his own. After making himself like them, he makes them like him. 'Then a pitiful faculty developed in their mind, that of perceiving stupidity and no longer tolerating it.' They become Flaubert at Croisset." [2]

Flaubert's intention "to vomit bile" on his contemporaries, to excoriate the swinishness of democratic bourgeois culture, likewise failed to materialize. The book cannot be read as an indictment of the nineteenth century. The contemporary setting, the realistic analysis of character and manners give the story its life in time and place; but the incredible succession of disasters and disillusionments which overtake the heroes can hardly be considered peculiar to a given era or civilization. The major catastrophes of the story are simply not the consequences either of bourgeois philistinism or of democratic materialism. Mr. Trilling's argument on this point is compelling. Things go wrong, partly, because Bouvard and Pécuchet are awkward little men who trip and stumble; partly, because of the very immensity of the data that their naïve curiosity undertakes to absorb; partly, because the author had determined that they should be comic characters who could never win.

More importantly, perhaps, we are involved in the disparity that separates idea from reality, in the difficulty of applying theory to situation, in the eternally losing struggle of mind against nature (Mr. Levin says of man and thing). Anyone who has tried to keep a lawn, or to raise a few tomato plants or zinnias in the backyard, knows that no matter how conscientiously he follows the prescriptions of the ever contradictory authorities, he must experience insect damage, fungus, and blight. Who has not despaired of finding comfort or certainty in a metaphysical system or in a religious dogma? Much nonsense has been written on education, but those who undertake to teach or to rear children learn quickly that sound theory often becomes simply irrelevant before the intractability of the material. This was the experience of the two clerks. But none of it was the fault of the nineteenth century or peculiar to the culture of Flaubert's bourgeois contemporaries. Mr. Trilling sums up the meaning of the novel thus:

> The more we consider *Bouvard and Pécuchet,* the less the novel can be thought of as nothing but an attack on the culture of the nineteenth century. Bourgeois democracy merely affords the setting for a situation in which it becomes possible to reject culture itself. The novel does nothing less than that: it rejects culture. The human mind experiences the massed accumulation of its own works, those that are traditionally held to be its greatest glories as well as those that are obviously of a contemptible sort, and arrives at the understanding that none will serve its purpose, that all are weariness and vanity, that the whole vast structure of human thought and creation are alien from the human person. Descharmes concludes his study of *Bouvard and Pécuchet* with the statement that the import of the novel is comprehended in a verse from Ecclesiastes which Flaubert might well have used as an epigraph: "And I set my mind to search and investigate through wisdom everything that is done beneath the heavens. It is an evil task that God has given the sons of men with which to occupy themselves." The relevance of the pessimism of Ecclesiastes goes well beyond this single text.
>
> The pessimism of *Bouvard and Pécuchet* is comparable with, although not the same as, that of *Gulliver's Travels.* Just as we may not lessen the depth of the pessimism of *Gulliver's Travels* by reading the book as if it were only Swift's response to the eighteenth century, so we may not lessen the depth of the pessimism of *Bouvard and Pécuchet* by reading it as if it were only Flaubert's response to the nineteenth century.
>
> What does permit us to qualify the pessimism of *Bouvard and Pécuchet* is the comic mode in which it has its existence. The book is genuinely funny, and the comic nature of the two heroes invites us to stand at a certain distance from their woe. . . . Bouvard and Pécuchet permit us to laugh at ourselves in them and yet remain detached from their plight. They are the *reductio ad absurdum* of our lives in culture, but we are not constrained to follow the reduction as far as it can take us.[3]

According to Albalat, the poet Heredia maintained that, if Flaubert could have finished *Bouvard et Pécuchet*, France would have had her *Don Quixote*. The same critic quotes Unamuno, who draws the same parallel and insists that the two clerks, like the knight and his servant, "are profoundly tragic" although "comic at first sight." [4] The effort of the two old bachelors to take human culture by storm had indeed its quixotic aspects, though both of Flaubert's heroes are far closer to the knight than they are to the squire. Could Gorju be given the role of Sancho Panza?

It is likewise possible to compare *Bouvard et Pécuchet* to *Candide*. The differences between the two works are many; but, like the two clerks, Voltaire's hero is beset by the refusal of life as it must be experienced in this world to conform to the categories in the terms of which philosophy and culture endeavor to describe it. Candide's effort to realize the best of possible worlds is quite as disastrous and perhaps even funnier than the failures of the experiments of Bouvard and Péchuchet. Flaubert expressed, throughout his life, the highest admiration for Voltaire's tale. In 1844, he claimed that he had read it more than twenty times and that he had translated it into English. (*Corr.*, I, 154) Thirty years later, when he was already engaged in the composition of *Bouvard et Pécuchet*, he wrote the following admonishment to the bereaved and discouraged Edmond de Goncourt:

How sad you are, my dear friend. Your discouragement distresses me. You are looking too deeply at things. When one reflects a trifle seriously, one is tempted to blow out his brain. That is why it is necessary to act. However stupid the book one is reading may be, it is important to finish it. The one that one is writing may be idiotic, no matter, write it. The end of *Candide*: "Let us cultivate our garden" is the greatest moral lesson that exists. (*Corr.*, VII, 202)

Had Flaubert lived to complete his novel he would have given to his heroes this consolation of work. It was this consolation that sustained him against the pessimism of his outlook and the tribulations of the last years of his life. When Bouvard and Pécuchet determine to abandon speculation and to "copier comme autrefois," they are very close to the serenity of Candide and his companions when they decide to "travailler sans penser." But, even though their copying is to point up the inadequacies of the intellect, they have not abandoned the life of the mind.

The reaction of the nineteenth century to *Bouvard et Pécuchet* was generally unfavorable. Even critics like Lanson and Faguet, who admired Flaubert's other work, were less than enthusiastic about his posthumous novel. Readers tended to find the characters boring, the erudition pedantic, the humor heavy. The twentieth century has treated the work more kindly. Albert Thibaudet, Rémy de Gourmont, and more recently Raymond Queneau have hailed it as a masterpiece. M. Dumesnil maintains that Bouvard and Pécuchet have the souls of apostles. Mr. Levin insists that we must be interested in them because "we are their heirs." Mr. Trilling would canonize the two copy clerks and give them a place in the company of Flaubert's saints.

CHAPTER 9

Testament of Youth

1.

"Je veux faire l'histoire morale des hommes de ma génération."

THE discussion of the *Education sentimentale* is reserved for the final chapter of this study because this novel constitutes Flaubert's most ambitious and most elaborate effort to portray contemporary bougeois society. The picture of the life of Paris in the decade of the 1840's with its multiple and varied aspects is drawn on a very broad canvas. It provides a most penetrating analysis of the social and political circumstances that produced the tragedy of the February Revolution and the reaction that followed it. It is the author's attempt to understand and to render the experience of his generation. To be the heroine and the symbol of this story of an unfulfilled love and of an unrealized ideal, Flaubert created his best drawn, most convincing, and most sympathetic character, Madame Arnoux.

Madame Bovary remains Flaubert's best-known, most widely read work. The vast preponderance of critical opinion reckons it his masterpiece and acclaims the book as one of the world's great novels. The *Education sentimentale* has never enjoyed this general esteem. Its failure, in 1869, before the public and the press was one of the great disappointments of Flaubert's life. While this first unfavorable reaction has been partially corrected with the passage of time, even today only a minority of readers know and love the *Education sentimentale*. There are some, nonetheless, who consider this work the author's supreme accomplishment; included in this group are René Dumesnil, Albert Thibaudet, and most recently Jean-Pierre Richard—some of the most perceptive, best-informed students of Flaubert. The author of the present study shares this opinion.

To find the earliest efforts, on the part of Flaubert, to treat the theme and a part of the subject matter of the *Education sentimentale*, we must return to the three autobiographical essays of his adolescence and youth which we described briefly in the closing paragraphs of Chapter Three. The plots of these tales show only scant resemblance to that of the novel of 1869, but the physical similarities of their heroines to Madame Arnoux and the efforts to apprehend the effect of the experience of love upon the several protagonists make it necessary to consider these early stories as prefigurations of the great work of the author's maturity.

A part of the *Mémoires d'un fou* may date from his sixteenth year, from 1838. Obviously inspired by Flaubert's experience with Madame Schlésinger, this novelette tells how the first-person protagonist, while on a beach that is obviously Trouville, met and fell hopelessly in love with a woman many years his senior. The circumstances of this encounter are similar to those in which Frédéric Moreau becomes enraptured of Madame Arnoux aboard the river steamer. The sentimental education of the hero of the *Mémoires* derives from his association with three highly literary and conceptual characters—the unattainable idol, the girl he might marry, and the prostitute. Here again, its relationship to the novel of 1869 is close.

For the purposes of this study, we might pass over *Novembre*, were it not for the fact that the boredom and world weariness of the hero suggest Frédéric during his law-school days. But the *Education sentimentale* (version of 1845) is clearly another youthful effort to handle the theme developed in the later work which bears the same title. Here, as we have seen, there are two heroes. Henri wins Emilie, elopes with her, tires of her; but he acquires from the experience aplomb, confidence, and worldly success. On the other hand, a disappointment in love leads Jules to abandon mundane concerns and to devote his energies and talents to study and literature. In the definitive *Education sentimentale*, the experiences of these two characters (and so much more) are combined in the story of Frédéric Moreau.

Rightly, Flaubert did not consider the first *Education* successful enough to publish. He put the manuscript away and produced, through the labor of seventeen years, the first *Saint-Antoine, Madame Bovary,* and *Salammbô.* It is interesting to note that on the completion of the Carthaginian novel in 1862 he considered giving definitive form to each of the three subjects that had obsessed him from youth to maturity. Should he re-write, once again, the *Tentation de Saint-Antoine,* begin *Bouvard et Pécuchet,* or endeavor to give fuller expression to the sentimental education theme? In due course, he settled upon the last possibility; and in October, 1864, he announced the beginning of the new project in a letter to Mademoiselle Leroyer de Chantepie:

For a month now, I have been harnessed to a novel of modern manners which will take place in Paris. I wish to write the moral history of the men of my generation, "sentimental" would be more accurate. It is a book of love, of passion; but of passion as it can exist now, that is, inactive. The subject, as I have conceived it, is, I believe, profoundly true, but for that very reason, probably not too amusing. (*Corr.,* V. 158)

The *Education sentimentale* is the story of the unfulfilled love of Frédéric Moreau and Madame Arnoux. Like the protagonist of the *Mémoires d'un fou,* the eighteen-year-old hero falls in love at first sight with the woman he sees sitting on the deck of the river boat. Shortly afterwards, as a law student in Paris, he finds it easy to win the confidence of her amiable but vulgar, philandering husband and to meet the family on intimate terms. For a period of many months, he pursues his legal studies without enthusiasm or energy, and worships Madame Arnoux in silence. This phase of the story reaches its culminating point at the end of Book I; after a gathering at the Arnoux house at St. Cloud, circumstance makes Frédéric a witness to her distress as she learns of one of her husband's infidelities. In a sort of complicity, they ride back to Paris together, alone in the carriage with the heroine's sleeping daughter.

Frédéric finishes his law course, returns home to Nogent-sur-Seine, and unwillingly accepts employment there in a law office. Then an inheritance from his uncle makes it possible for him to abandon his profession, to return to Paris, and to set himself up in the capital for a life of leisure. He again frequents the Arnoux, whose financial position is deteriorating. Arnoux introduces him to the courtesan, Rosanette. Through months of frustration, Frédéric pays vain court to the two women. He wins Madame Arnoux' confidence, but she refuses to understand and surrounds herself with her children when he tries to declare his love. Rosanette seems to encourage him, but she simply laughs when his advances reach a certain point. In despair, Frédéric gives serious consideration to marrying his Nogent neighbor, little Louise Roque. Madame Arnoux learns of this proposal, becomes jealous, and begins a new phase in her relationship to Frédéric. Through the fall of 1847, the two hold idyllic but platonic trysts in a house at Auteuil. These moments are those of their greatest intimacy.

The hero now resolves to possess his idol by fraud or by force. He rents an apartment on the rue Tronchet and imagines a ruse to lead Madame Arnoux into it. The illness of her son prevents her from keeping the rendezvous. As the Revolution of 1848 unleashes itself in Paris, Frédéric, angry and humiliated, seeks out Rosanette and takes her into the bower he had prepared with such devotion for his beloved.

In Part III, during the early days of the Second Republic, the hero and the courtesan lead a carefree life together. But Frédéric cannot forget his dream. In the winter of 1849, he calls on the idol again. All is explained and forgiven; and it appears, once more, that the couple is about to unite when their conversation is interrupted by the appearance of Rosanette, who has come to the apartment because she has business with Arnoux. This development, more symbolic than credible, indicates clearly that the hero's new involvements make it impossible for him to pursue any longer his dream.

But Frédéric's sentimental education is not yet complete. When the hero, without breaking with Rosanette, becomes the lover of Madame Dambreuse, the lessons taught by the idol, the courtesan, and the marriageable girl are completed by the wealthy, aristocratic woman of the world. When Monsieur Dambreuse dies, the two plan to marry; and Frédéric seems about to be carried to position and great wealth. The reaction has set in.

Meanwhile, the Arnoux flounder toward bankruptcy. Both Madame Dambreuse and Rosanette are jealous of the idol. In a complicated intrigue, both obtain legal judgments against her which make her financial catastrophe complete. Despite Frédéric's effort to rescue them, the Arnoux must take flight. They are driven out of Paris and out of the hero's life. In loyalty to Madame Arnoux, he abandons Rosanette and breaks his engagement to Madame Dambreuse. It is December 2, 1851, the day of Louis Napoleon's *coup d'état.*

Frédéric traveled. He came back: "He frequented society, and he had still other loves. But the continual memory of the first one made them seem insipid; and then the vehemence of desire, the very flower of sensation, were lost. His intellectual ambitions had likewise diminished. Years passed; and he endured the idleness of his intelligence and the inertia of his heart." (*L'Education senti-mentale,* 600) Then, sixteen years later, in March, 1867, a white-haired woman calls at Frédéric's apartment. They discuss their youth and recall the incidents of their overwhelming but unful-filled love. They take a walk together through the Paris streets. Back in the apartment, she cuts off a lock of her hair, presents it to Frédéric, and says good-bye. Frédéric goes to the window and watches her get into a cab. "Et ce fut tout."

The background against which this story unfolds is dense, de-tailed, and varied. The protagonists are surrounded by a large group of sharply etched secondary characters; the Paris in which the action takes place is so real that the reader sees the streets and the crowds, feels the asphalt under his feet; the care and skill with which history is treated make the novel one of the most important books we have on the last years of Louis-Philippe and the Febru-ary Revolution. In a very real sense, it is Flaubert's testament of his youth and his account of the age in which he spent it.

The sources of the *Education sentimentale* lie deep in Flau-bert's most intimate experience. It is obvious that Madame Arnoux is a portrait of Madame Schlésinger and that the story of Fréd-éric's love for her is inspired by the author's worship of the music publisher's wife. Could there be any lingering doubt about these facts, it would be dissipated by the earliest outlines of the novel in one of the author's *carnets,* in which he notes that the characters will be "Mme Sch—— M. Sch—— moi." [1] Many of the scenes be-tween the two protagonists had doubtless occurred many years before the novel was written in the course of the courtship by Flaubert of his beloved.

We must nonetheless resist the temptation to read the story as an autobiography or a confession. We are dealing with a novelist and not a reporter; we are not justified in assuming that the plot of the book follows the events of real life. Indeed, we know that frequently it does not. The author transmutes, transposes, and rearranges his memories for artistic effect. Thus the ride back to Paris from St. Cloud, where Frédéric and Madame Arnoux are alone in the carriage with little Marie sleeping between them, is the evocation of a similar ride in the Bois de Boulogne, but the author was not with Elisa Schlésinger; he was with Louise Colet and her daughter. (*Corr.* I, 273) The opening scene on board the "Ville de Montereau" recalls a boat trip Flaubert made with his mother in 1853, and the detail of the shawl that threatens to slide into the water was perhaps suggested by an incident of an earlier boat trip with Le Poittevin, in 1838. (*Corr.*, III, 331 and 332)

The characters likewise are composites. Frédéric Moreau must certainly be associated with Flaubert, not only in the nature of his feeling for Madame Arnoux, but also in the tedium and boredom of his law-school days as described in Part I of the novel. But nothing in the author's life suggests the rich young man about town of Parts II and III. Like Frédéric, Flaubert traveled, but he did not come back "to endure the idleness of his intelligence." And when the hero woos and wins Madame Dambreuse in Part III, we are reminded, not of an incident in the life of the author, but of the affair between Maxime Du Camp and Madame Delessert. Moreau, then, is both Flaubert and Du Camp—and perhaps many other persons as well. Features that suggest Du Camp can likewise be found in Deslauriers (his ambition, his admiration for Rastignac), and perhaps in the painter, Pellerin, who ends his career as a photographer, although Du Camp himself thought this artist was a portrait of Nadar.

The charming professional, Rosanette, *la Maréchale,* is drawn in part after Madame Sabatier, *la Présidente,* who inspired some of Baudelaire's finest poems, and whose drawing-room Flaubert frequented in the 1860's. But the story of her sad initiation into prostitution was supplied by the actress Suzanne Lagier. We are justified, I believe, in associating Louise Roque, or at least some of the incidents in which she is involved, with Gertrude Collier. Louise likewise suggests the English girl in the *Mémoires d'un fou,* who is generally supposed to be inspired by Gertrude. Every-

thing we know about Maurice Schlésinger attests that the remarkable portrait of the generous unscrupulous wastrel and sensualist
Jacques Arnoux is a striking likeness. For reasons that appear to
me very inadequate, critics have associated the novelist, Prosper
Mérimée, with Martinon. We are perhaps closer to the truth if we
think of Flaubert's school confidant, Ernest Chevalier. Like Martinon, Chevalier quickly outgrew the extravagance of his youth,
became a prudent bourgeois, had a conventional legal career, and
ended his life a senator. Flaubert's letter to his mother, when he
learned of Chevalier's marriage, describes Martinon quite as well
as it does his boyhood companion. (*Corr.*, II, 269) These associa-
tions are legitimate and illuminating. They throw light both on
the background of the book and on the operation of the creative
process within the author's mind. They mislead us only if we tend
to consider the novel a *roman à clef.*

2.

"ce bon air de Paris"

These characters and the many others that the book presents
move—sometimes together, sometimes apart—through incidents
and scenes which permit the author to picture the streets of Paris
and to study countless aspects and phases of the life of the city.
Frédéric, particularly during his law-school days, tramps continually through the capital and gives us sometimes quick glimpses
of the animation of the boulevards, sometimes carefully wrought
descriptions of the carriages on the Champs-Elysées or the sun
setting under the Arc de Triomphe after a sudden shower. The
night of his first invitation to dinner at the Arnoux apartment, he
walks home to the Quai Napoléon (now the Quai de la Corse) on
the Cité, thinking disdainfully of the people sleeping behind those
walls who existed without seeing Madame Arnoux. He reaches the
river: "The street lights shone in two straight lines, blurredly, and
long, red flames flickered in the depth of the water. It was slate
colored while the sky, lighter, seemed to be sustained by the great
masses of shadow which rose on each side of the river. Buildings,
which one could not make out, doubled the darkness. A luminous
mist floated above, on the roofs. All the noises melted into a single

drone; a light wind was blowing." (*L'Education sentimentale*, 71)

There is also the winter morning when Frédéric, after receiving his inheritance, returns to Paris by stagecoach. He is riding in along the quais near the Jardin des Plantes. The river is swollen:

> The Seine, yellowish, almost touched the roadway of the bridges. It exhaled a freshness. Frédéric breathed it in with all his strength, relishing this good air of Paris which seems to contain effluviums of love and intellectual emanations; he was touched when he saw the first cab. And he loved even the thresholds of the wine merchants strewn with straw, even the street cleaners with their boxes, even the grocer boys shaking their coffee roasters. Women were trotting under umbrellas; he leaned out to distinguish their faces; a chance might have brought out Madame Arnoux.   (148)

There is the description of the hippodrome at the Champs-de-Mars, the Sunday in May, 1847, when Frédéric escorted Rosanette to the races. We see the crowds, the carriages; the horses on the far side of the track seem to move slowly and scarcely touch the ground; when they pass nearby, the earth trembles and pebbles fly; the air balloons the colored jackets of the jockeys.

Rosanette is also the center of the scene which describes the masked ball in her apartments shortly after Frédéric's return to Paris. Flaubert, here, was perhaps thinking of the orgy in Balzac's *Peau de Chagrin;* but he obtains very different effects with a far more consummate art. The impression is that of a painting by Renoir, in which forms merge indistinctly one with the other, and colors are transformed by the play of light: "Frédéric was dazzled at first by the lights; he made out only silk, velvet, bare shoulders, a mass of colors which swayed to the sound of an orchestra hidden by green plants, between walls lined in yellow silk, with pastel portraits here and there, and crystal candelabras in Louis XVI style. High lamps, whose frosted globes resembled snowballs, dominated baskets of flowers, placed on pier tables in the corners." (164) The frivolity of this all night orgy has its undertones of tragedy; its gaiety is superficial, its intoxication ephemeral. But Frédéric is dazzled; the ball becomes the symbol of that glittering Parisian life he is determined to experience; the motley confusion of women in masquerade awakes in the hero new ambitions and new desires:

Another thirst had come over him, one for women, luxury, and everything that Parisian life calls forth. He felt a bit giddy, like a man who gets off a ship; and in the hallucination of his first sleep, he saw passing back and forth continually, the shoulders of the Fishwife, the loins of the Docker woman, the calves of the Polish girl, the hair of the Savage. Then two big black eyes, which were not at the ball, appeared; and light as butterflies, ardent as torches, they came, went, shimmered, rose to the cornice, came down as far as his mouth. Frédéric struggled to recognize these eyes, without succeeding.   (183)

Momentarily obscured by the confusion, make-believe, and motley of the courtesan's masked ball, the hero's ideal becomes unrecognizable.

3.

"Si l'on avait compris L'Education sentimentale, *tout cela ne serait pas arrivée."*

The analysis of the social and political history of the decade preceding the *coup d'état* of 1851 is treated in detail quite as abundant and specific as the physical aspects of the life of Paris. The characters of the novel witness and sometimes share the political passions of the period. A large part of Part III is devoted to the Revolution of 1848 and the tribulations of the Second Republic. But in the earlier parts of the story, the tensions that were dividing France in the twilight of the Bourgeois Monarchy are evident in the differences of opinion expressed in the gatherings of the several groups of characters. The *cénacle* of students and young intellectuals that surrounds Frédéric is revolutionary in outlook. The prudent, generally aged businessmen who frequent the salon of Monsieur and Madame Dambreuse are complacent and therefore impatient about any proposal for change or reform. Unimportant and frequently forgotten items of the news of the day provide the subject matter of many of these dialogues. To be sure that the events under discussion were authentic and appeared in their proper chronological context, the author examined and took notes from the files of countless periodicals and newspapers of the epoch he was treating.

As Flaubert himself could not live and work without a confidant, he provided Frédéric Moreau with an *alter ego*, albeit one who was at times unreliable and disloyal, in the person of Charles Deslauriers. The novel devotes many pages to the warmth of their youthful friendship and their life together. They quarrel and separate, they betray each other, but their intimacy is always resumed. The closing chapter of the book pictures them together by the fire, discussing the events of their youth, "reconciled once more by a fatality of their nature which made them always come back together and love each other."

Deslauriers, a lawyer, is intelligent, ambitious, and impoverished. He blames the establishment for his inability to push to a position of power and wealth and he is eloquent and articulate in his attacks on the régime. The two friends gather about them a group composed of the office employee, Dussardier, who hates oppression; Hussonnet, the frivolous bohemian journalist; Sénécal, the dogmatic socialist intellectual and others: "All sympathized. First of all, their hatred of the Goverment had the elevation of a dogma that could not be discussed. Only Martinon tried to defend Louis-Philippe. They heaped upon him commonplaces that filled the newspapers: the fortification of Paris, the September laws, Pritchard, Lord Guizot,—so much so that Martinon stopped talking, fearing to offend someone." (80)

The revolutionary fervor of these young men reaches its height in September, 1847, at a gathering at Dussardier's. Drinks were flowing—"and they were not long in becoming excited, all feeling the same exasperation against the Power. It was violent, without other cause than hatred of injustice; and they mixed with legitimate griefs, the stupidest reproaches." (378)

Dussardier, destined to be killed as he shouts "Vive la Republique" at the moment of the *coup d'état*, is one of the most appealing and most wholly decent characters in the novel:

One day, when he was fifteen, on la rue Transnonain, in front of a grocer's shop, he had seen soldiers, their bayonets red with blood, with hair clinging to the stock of their rifles; since that time the Government had exasperated him as the very incarnation of injustice. He confused assassins somewhat with policemen; a spy, in his eyes, was on the same level as a parricide. All the evil flowing over the earth he attributed naïvely to Authority. He hated it with an essential, permanent hatred, which filled his whole heart and refined his sensibility.   (333)

The contrast to these conversations among the angry young men is provided by the scenes in the Dambreuse salon. Frédéric and Martinon, who frequent both groups, are our links between these two worlds. Monsieur Dambreuse, the great capitalist of the novel, is perhaps the symbol of the men who composed the government under the Bourgeois Monarchy. He organizes vast corporations involved in railroading and coal mining. He knows that the Industrial Revolution has at last reached France, and he also knows how to profit from it. Naturally enough, he is surrounded by men devoted to the *status quo,* and frightened by anything that seems to threaten its tiniest detail. Two examples fix the tone of these conversations:

Now it [the conversation] was concerned with pauperism, all the pictures of which, according to these gentlemen, were highly exaggerated.

"Nonetheless," objected Martinon, "poverty exists, let's confess it. But the remedy lies neither with Science or the Government. It's a purely individual question. When the lower classes are willing to get rid of their vices, they will free themselves of their needs. Let the people be more moral, and they won't be so poor." (339)

In the course of the same evening,

An industrialist, a former carbonaro, tried to point out to him that the d'Orleans were a fine family; doubtless these were abuses. . . .

"Well, then?"

"But one must not mention them, dear sir. If you knew how all these railings of the opposition hurt business." (343)

Flaubert is not gentle with these conservatives, but neither is he very kind to the radicals. In a pronouncement which departs from the impersonality he extolls and reveals a personal judgment, he declares: "Most of the men who were there had served at least four governments; and they would have sold France, or the human kind, to guarantee their fortune, to spare themselves a discomfort, an embarrassment, or even out of simple baseness, instinctive adoration of power. All declared political crimes inexcusable." (342) The revolution is not far off.

The tableaux of the February days, of the Paris streets in the first intoxication of the republican victory, and of the reaction that followed June are among the most impressive pages of the novel. We see these events, not as the social scientist would present them, in orderly sequence of cause and effect, but as they appeared to the men and women who witnessed them or who participated on the fringes of the action. The leaders who made the important decisions—the Guizots, the Lamartines, and the rest—remain in the background. We are shown the bewildering succession of events, in the multiplicity of its specific and frequently irrational and incongruous detail. With Frédéric, we walk through the streets of Paris on February 22nd and 23rd; but he is much more concerned with his sentimental problems than with the events. On the 22nd, Madame Arnoux fails to keep the appointment; on the 23rd, he takes vengeance by possessing Rosanette. On the 24th, he watches the fighting at the Palais-Royal and follows the mob into the Tuileries. Through his eyes, and those of Rosanette, we see the gaiety of the town in the morning glow of the Republic. The incredible stupidity of the discussions and tirades at the *Club de l'Intelligence* follows.

Because Frédéric and Rosanette spend three days at Fontaine-bleau, we miss the June riots. The hero returns to nurse the wounded Dussardier only after the laborers have been beaten and suppressed. The violence of the reaction appears in the frightening scene in which *le père* Roque fires into the crowd of prisoners massed in the basement of the *terrase au bord de l'eau* and in the bitterness of the conversation at the dinner party at the Dambreuse residence.

The authenticity and accuracy of these scenes is beyond dispute. Flaubert had himself witnessed many of the events he describes. He and Du Camp had been present at the fighting in the Palais-Royal and had entered the Tuileries with the first of the revolutionaries. But he did not rely on his memory alone. He made extensive use of such works as Daniel Stern's *Histoire de la Révolution de 1848;* he absorbed countless contemporary pamphlets and brochures; he worked through the files of a large part of the Paris press. All of the details reported are founded on fact. All of the incongruous absurdities and nonsense of the meeting of the *Club de l'Intelligence* can be documented. The author had a source for every example of the ferocity and panic of the victorious bourgeoisie after the rebellion of June. He is as severe toward the dogmatic stupidity of the socialists as toward the bad faith and duplicity of the conservatives:

Equality (as if to punish its defenders and deride its enemies) made itself triumphantly manifest, an equality of brute beasts; a single level of bloody turpitudes; for the fanaticism of self-interest balanced the delirium of want, the aristocracy had the passions of the mob, and the cotton night cap showed itself no less hideous than the red bonnet. Public reason was troubled as after the great upheavals of nature. Because of it, intelligent people remained idiots for the rest of their lives. (483)

This is the novelist's conclusion concerning the events of June. Flaubert penned this plague on both houses in 1867 or '68. Was he aware that June, 1848, had opened between proletarian and bourgeois in France an abyss of hatred which the passage of more than one hundred years has not entirely closed? In any case, he has left us what may be the finest account of the upheaval. This novel is also a historical study of rare, unusual insight and excellence.

4.

"montrer que le Sentimentalisme suit la Politique et en reproduit les phases."

We are now in a position to appreciate the wondrous unity of this dense, detailed, and remarkable book. The author's historical erudition is broad and sound. The historical material, however, is more than a picturesque backdrop against which the characters live their lives. It is a completely integral part of the story which augments, confirms, and illumines the experience of the protagonists. Frédéric can never win the only woman he is capable of loving, and upon this underlying assumption the *Education sentimentale* is based. The hero's efforts to seize and possess the ideal which Madame Arnoux incarnates inevitably fails; and the failure forces him to settle for the insipid satisfactions that can be realized in the world of action. History tells the same story in this novel: France's attempt to achieve Utopia through revolution leads likewise to disaster. The two themes are so complementary, so interwoven, that they become one and the same.

Personal aspirations parallel political passions. Early in 1848, after the idyllic meetings between the hero and his beloved at Auteuil, the moment comes when Frederic can no longer endure the chastity of his attachment:

Her return to Paris, and the complications of New Year's Day, suspended for a bit their interviews. When he came back, there was something more forward in his manner. She left the room at every minute to give orders, and received, despite his plea, all the callers who came to see her. Then they indulged in conversation about Léotade, M. Guizot, the Pope, the insurrection at Palermo, and the banquet of the XIIth arrondissement, which was causing anxiety. Frédéric relieved himself by heaping abuse upon the Government; for he wished, like Deslauriers, for a universal upheaval, so embittered was he now. Madame Arnoux, on her side, became somber. (393)

Unable to bear his frustration, the hero resolves upon a ruse, almost an abduction. Madame Arnoux consents to his desire for her to meet him and walk with him along the rue Tronchet; Frédéric rents an apartment into which he means to lead her and furnishes with loving care the rooms which are to receive her. But the ideal cannot be possessed by ruse and force; and, in the bower he had so lovingly prepared, Frédéric embraces, not Madame Arnoux, but the venal Rosanette: "The flowers had not faded. The lace cover was spead on the bed. He brought the little slippers out of the closet. Rosanette found these attentions very delicate. At about one o'clock she was awakened by distant rumblings; and she saw him sobbing, with his head buried in the pillow." (408) It is the twenty-third of February. Other idealists are resorting to violence and manning the barricades. Like Madame Arnoux, Utopia failed to keep the appointment; France found herself, instead, involved with the ill-starred Republic of 1848.

Rosanette is not simply the woman with whom Frédéric betrayed his dream; she is also the Revolution. The hero's contact with her involves him, inevitably, in a succession of actions that blur and destroy the dream. The intimacy of the trysts at Auteuil can never be resumed. It is not that Madame Arnoux is unable to forgive. When Frédéric seeks her again, she is ready to pardon and forget all. But Rosanette takes back her lover. "Pourquoi vas-tu te divertir chez les femmes honnêtes?" She has claims upon him; she is about to bear his son. And the illegitimate offspring of the protagonist and the courtesan proves no more viable than the Republic born of the irresponsibility and violence of the February Revolution.

If Rosanette is the personification of the Revolution, Frédéric's affair and engagement with Madame Dambreuse becomes the parable of the Reaction. In the banker's salon, the hero saw at close hand the political leaders of the day:

He was stupified by their execrable language, their pettiness, their rancors, their bad faith, all these people who had voted for the Constitution doing their utmost to destroy it. . . . Political verbiage and good food numbed his morality. As mediocre as these personages appeared to him, he was proud to know them and within himself, he wished for bourgeois consideration. A mistress like Madame Dambreuse would set him up. (521 ff)

He was surprised at the facility with which he won her. But, like the politicians struggling to destroy the Constitution they had sworn to uphold, Frédéric continued his liaison with Rosanette and his life became a web of deceptions and untruths: "Soon these lies amused him; he repeated to one the oath that he had just made to the other, sent them two identical bouquets, wrote to them at the same time, then established comparisons between them; there was a third always present in his thought. The impossibility of having her justified him in his perfidies." (557)

In a revealing insight, Monsieur Richard has observed that Frédéric's conduct here would be incomprehensible if he had loved either of the women or if he had loved them both. It is the absence of Madame Arnoux, to which we shall return, which gives the situation its meaning. Had there been any loyalty, any enthusiasm for either the Republic, or the sort of Restoration which her politicians were seeking, the transactions which led to the *coup d'état* would have been impossible.

Madame Dambreuse had her faults:

Her way of playing the piano was correct and harsh. Her spiritualism (Madame Dambreuse believed in the transmigration of souls in the stars) did not prevent her from keeping her books admirably. She was haughty with her servants; her eyes remained dry before the rags of the poor. An ingenuous egoism burst forth in her ordinary locutions: "What difference does that make to me? I would be too kind; what need have I?"—and a thousand little unanalyzable, odious actions. She would have listened behind doors; she must have lied to her confessor. Out of spirit of domination, she wanted Frédéric to accompany her on Sunday to church. He obeyed, and carried the book. (559)

But she had wealth, position, and fashion on her side; she would doubtless have won out over Rosanette's naturalness and youth.

However, neither woman could make the hero forget the dream, the absence in which he had his being. They could and did drive Madame Arnoux out of Paris, but when, that afternoon in December, 1851, Madame Dambreuse attempted to purchase the secret of the little box with silver corners and clasps, Frédéric effected his own *coup d'état*.

Ingenious and labored parallels which the author never intended? I believe not. Certainly the juxtaposition of personal and political crisis is not mere coincidence. And there is a curious sentence in the *carnet* in which Flaubert jotted his earliest plans for the novel: "Show that Sentimentalism (its development since 1830) follows Politics and reproduces its phases." [2] Cryptic as these words are, we are justified in concluding that the author intended that the love story should follow and interpret the course of political events. According to Maxime Du Camp, it is also a fact that Flaubert attached great social significance to the novel. Flaubert said to his friend, as they gazed, in 1871 after the suppression of the Commune, on the ruins of the Tuileries, "If people had understood the *Education sentimentale*, all that would not have happened." [3]

It is thus that the novelist reveals himself historian and the erudite scholar to be an artist. He imposes the order and logic of art upon the complex and contradictory phenomena of the February Revolution and the *Coup d'état*—and without falsifying or deforming them. Fiction interprets the political events while history enriches and illuminates the plot. Fiction and history tell a same story and reach a same conclusion.

5.

"Et ce fut comme une apparition."

The *Education sentimentale* finds its unity and meaning in the emanation of the beauty of Madame Arnoux. From the moment she appears on the deck of the boat steaming from Paris to Nogent, Frédéric's world assumes new dimension and perspective. People and things acquire significance and reason for being in terms of the beloved and as intermediaries between him and her: "The contemplation of that woman enervated him, like the use of too strong a perfume. It descended to the depths of his temperament, and became almost a general way of feeling, a new mode of existing." (97)

Frédéric became aware of other women because they resembled or were unlike her. Articles of clothing were on display in show windows only so that he could imagine them on her person. A palm tree at the Jardin des Plantes made him dream of traveling with her in exotic climes. He substituted her likeness for the personages in the paintings at the Louvre. "All streets led to her house, carriages stood in the squares only to take one there faster; Paris was related to her person, and the great city, with all its voices, sounded, like an immense orchestra, around her." (97)

Madame Arnoux is the luminous point at which all lines converge. She is the mystery which lies beyond and at the end of every sensation and reflection. She is, to quote Monsieur Richard, the void and the secret in terms of which the objects of this world are oriented:

So the *Education sentimentale* is first of all the novel of absence, of a reality which steals itself away, and concerning which the hero finally accepts the fact that it will always escape him. . . . No one, not even the reader, can directly seize what makes up her essence. We hear her move behind a partition, we glimpse her profile behind a drapery: one can never possess more than her echo or than her shadow. Screens, fans, lampshades, her house is full of interposing objects. . . . Everything at Mme Arnoux' is sheltered behind partitions and veils. Doors close, curtains fall, we see the hem of a dress slip by or we smell a trace of perfume; everything closes and retires in the penumbra in which she likes to conceal her face. One would say that she is protecting a secret. And the little box, always closed, which passes from her to Rosanette, then that Madame Dambreuse wants to buy at the auction, represents admirably that forbidden portion, that treasure which no one is permitted to look upon in full light. To open the box would therefore be tantamount to a rape, a profanation; and that is indeed the reason for which Madame Dambreuse wishes to procure it for herself, the reason also for which Frédéric breaks with her. He cannot consent to the destruction, even symbolic, of this void upon which his entire life is founded.[4]

Tender and chaste, proud and modest, noble and suffering, Madame Arnoux walks in beauty. The mystery of her essence, the secret of the ideal she incarnates casts its light over every person and every object in the world that she inhabits. She has only to appear, and the normally closed universe opens up to the aspirations of human longing. Yet she remains appealingly feminine and human.

It is curious and interesting to note that it was not thus that Flaubert first conceived his heroine. The earliest sketches of the novel, as recorded in *carnet 19*, reveal that the author's first intention was to let Frédéric win Madame Arnoux and to make the novel the story of a banal and disappointing adultery.[5] Only bit by bit is the heroine idealized; only after long meditation and effort did the author glimpse the central idea of an unrealized love. The process by which the novelist came upon the true nature of his characters was long and arduous. It is almost as if Flaubert had meant to tell another story and as if Madame Arnoux, in her chaste beauty, had imposed herself upon his will. Did art embellish reality here, or was the memory of the great love of Flaubert's life so powerful that the story had to be told in its touching incompleteness and simplicity?

The novel has been criticized because most of the characters are failures or, at best, lead uneventful and inglorious lives. Maxime Du Camp proposed the title, *Les Gens médiocres*. But, despite her vicissitudes and defeats, Madame Arnoux is far from mediocre; and Frédéric, who lacks ambition and cannot "suivre la ligne droite," lives nonetheless in a world ennobled by love and art. The fact is that all but the most favored among us settle for mediocre existences. Ford Madox Ford is not far wrong when he insists that no one can consider himself educated until he has read the "thrice blessed *Education sentimentale*" fourteen times.

CHAPTER 10

Conclusion

BETWEEN 1830 and 1850, Stendhal and Balzac had brought to the novel new depth and acuity of psychological insight and a vast new breadth of sociological scope. The work of the former was generally ignored by his own generation and the one that followed him. The impact of the *Comédie humaine,* on the other hand, was immediate and profound. When Balzac died, in 1850, a number of young men of mediocre talent aspired to the mantle of the master and endeavored to carry on his work. One of these, who used the pen name Champfleury, led a journalistic campaign which made the first wide use of the word *realism* in literary criticism. Indeed, Champfleury consecrated himself the high priest of the new Realistic school of novelists. The point here is not the fact that these young writers displayed little talent; it is rather that the example and influence of Balzac appeared to be leading to a novel which would strive exclusively for the photographic reproduction of the most banal and ordinary reality. In this pursuit, considerations of form, style, and artistic effect were of minimal importance. The novel was to become a sort of journalism which would pretend to truth at the expense of beauty. It was the publication of *Madame Bovary* that revealed the hollowness of this conception and opened rich new perspectives to Realism and the novel.

Flaubert's admiration for Balzac was genuine and profound. He was moved and impressed by the power and scope of the *Comédie humaine,* and he was fully aware of the greatness of his predecessor's accomplishment. He was repelled, however, by the clumsy composition and awkward expression that characterize some of the great novelist's finest work: "What a man Balzac would have been if he had known how to write." (*Corr.,* III, 68)

To the Realistic and visionary power of Balzac, Flaubert sought to bring the added dimension of perfected form and narrative technique. Writing, even the writing of prose fiction to describe a middle-class setting, was an art; and the creation of an appropriate style could give to the novel a beauty and dignity in the hierarchy of literary forms that it had not yet attained. Fully aware of the importance of the accomplishment of Balzac, Flaubert was unwilling to abandon, however, values he saw in the stylistic creatures of his Romantic forebears: Chateaubriand, Hugo, and Gautier (not to mention Shakespeare, Rabelais, and his favorite Latin authors). The novel, as Flaubert envisaged and practiced it, was to retain virtues of both literary currents. It was to combine the strength and the Realistic pretensions of Balzac and the evocative and poetic power of Chateaubriand. Flaubert invented, for the description of bourgeois society, an artistic, even an epic prose, which was none the less appropriate to the subject. Herein lie his originality and his greatness.

In Flaubert we find the most complete and the most genial expression of the several tendencies that distinguished the disillusioned, post-1848 period in France. This age exalted erudition and science; it believed in materialistic determinism. In these respects, Flaubert's novels were sufficiently impressive to compel the admiration of Taine himself. In the artistic realm, the age sought new techniques and formal perfection. Here, Flaubert stands superior to Leconte de Lisle, the Goncourt brothers, and Gautier; and he remains the peer of Baudelaire.

The next generation of novelists—Zola, Daudet, and Maupassant—considered themselves disciples of the master of Croisset; but they seem to have given more attention to his Realistic than to his stylistic techniques. It was Henry James, who called him "the novelist's novelist," who primarily employed and developed Flaubert's artistic inventions. From James, the mantle fell to Proust and Joyce. Flaubert's contribution to the history of the novel, in France and in the West, is of capital importance. And the legendary study at Croisset, the life-long struggle to apprehend Truth through Beauty, remains an inspiration to all who believe in the dignity of the artist's calling.

Notes and References

CHAPTER TWO

1. *Oeuvres complètes de Gustave Flaubert* (Paris, 1909-53); *Correspondance*, IV, 234. Unless otherwise specified, all references to Flaubert texts are to this edition. I have made my own translations.
2. Anthony Thorlby, *Gustave Flaubert and the Art of Realism* (London, 1956), p. 11.
3. René de Weck, "L'Ascétisme de Flaubert," *Mercure de France,* May 15, 1930.
4. Jean-Pierre Richard, "La Création de la forme chez Flaubert," in *Littérature et Sensation* (Paris, 1954), p. 205.
5. This chapter was ready for the press when B. F. Bart's excellent article, "Flaubert's Concept of the Novel" (PMLA, March, 1965), came to my attention. I am in essential agreement with Mr. Bart's contentions.

CHAPTER THREE

1. Jean Bruneau, *Les Débuts littéraires de Gustave Flaubert: 1831-1845* (Paris, 1962), p. 9.

CHAPTER FOUR

1. Maxime Du Camp, *Souvenirs littéraires* (Paris, 1906), Chapter xii.
2. (New York, 1963), pp. 231-45.

CHAPTER FIVE

1. Quoted by Jacques Suffel, *Gustave Flaubert* (Paris, 1958), p. 36.
2. "She remained a few minutes holding between her fingers this coarse paper. The mistakes in spelling were tangled one in the other,

and Emma pursued the tender thought that clucked through them like a hen half hidden in a thorny hedge. The writing had been dried with ashes from the fireplace, for a little gray dust slipped from the letter to her dress, and she believed almost that she saw her father bending toward the hearth to seize the tongs. How long it was since she had been with him, on the stool, by the fireplace, when she used to light the end of a stick from the bright flame of sparkling furse. . . . She remembered summer evenings bright with sunlight. The colts would neigh when one passed, and kept galloping, galloping. . . . There was a hive under her window, and sometimes the bees, whirling in the light, would strike against the pane like bounding balls of gold. What happiness at that time. What freedom. What hope. What an abundance of illusions. No more of them remained now. She had expended them in all the adventures of her soul, through all her successive conditions, in virginity, in marriage, and in love; losing them thus continually throughout her life, like a traveler who leaves something of his wealth at each of the inns along the way."

3. Jean Pommier, *Créations en littérature* (Paris, 1957), p. 15.

<h3 style="text-align:center">CHAPTER SIX</h3>

1. *Die Berührung der Sphären* (Berlin, 1931), p. 141 (quoted by Levin).

2. "The moon rose skimming the waves, and, over the town, still covered with darkness, bright points, white spots gleamed: the shaft of a cart in a yard, some hanging bit of cloth, the corner of a wall, a golden collar on the breast of a god. The glass balls on the roofs of the temples shone, here and there, like big diamonds. But vague ruins, heaps of dark earth, gardens, formed more somber masses in the darkness; and down at Malqua, fisherman's nets stretched from one house to the next, like gigantic bats unfolding their wings. One no longer heard the creaking of the hydraulic wheels which pumped water to the highest floors of the palaces, and in the midst of the terraces the camels were resting peacefully, lying on their stomachs, like ostriches. The porters slept in the streets propped against the thresholds of houses; colossal shadows crossed the deserted squares; in the distance sometimes the smoke of a still burning sacrifice rose from bronze flues, and the heavy breeze carried, along with aromatic perfumes, marine odors, and the exhalation of the walls heated by the sun. Around Carthage, the motionless waves glistened, for the moon cast her glow at once on the gulf surrounded by mountains and on the lake of Tunis, where flamingos in the sand banks formed long pink lines, while be-

yond, beneath the catacombs, the salt lagoon shimmered like a piece of silver. The vault of the blue sky grew darker at the horizon, on one side in the powder of the plains, on the other in the mists of the sea, and on the summit of the Acropolis, the pyramidal cypress trees, lining the temple of Eshmun swayed and murmured, like the waves which beat slowly and steadily along the breakwater, below the ramparts."

3. *Corréspondance générale* (Conard edition), XV, 129.

CHAPTER SEVEN

1. "He knew hunger, thirst, fever, and vermin. He grew accustomed to the din of the fray, to the aspect of the dying. The wind tanned his skin. His members were hardened by the contact of armor; and as he was very strong, courageous, temperate, circumspect, he obtained without difficulty the command of a company.

"Fugitive slaves, peasants in revolt, bastards with no fortune, all sorts of intrepid men thronged under his flag, and he formed an army.

"It grew larger. He became famous. People sought him out.

"He went off, begging his way through the world.

"He held out his hand to horsemen on the roads, with genuflections he approached harvesters, or remained motionless in front of farmyard gates; and his face was so sad that he was never refused alms."

2. Quoted from René Dumesnil, Preface to his edition of *Trois Contes* (Paris, 1957), p. LXIV.

3. Ford Madox Ford, *Between Saint Dennis and Saint George* (London, 1915), p. 203.

CHAPTER EIGHT

1. Quoted by Jacques Suffel, *Gustave Flaubert* (Paris, 1958), p. 112.

2. *Gustave Flaubert* (Paris, 1935).

3. Lionel Trilling, *The Opposing Self* (New York, 1955), p. 195.

4. Antoine Albalat, *Gustave Flaubert et ses amis* (Paris, 1927), p. 83.

CHAPTER NINE

1. This *carnet* has been published by Marie-Jeanne Durry, *Flaubert et ses projets inédits* (Paris, 1950). See especially pp. 123 ff.

2. *Ibid.*, p. 187. Madame Durry's reading of this page does not

show that Flaubert inadvertantly wrote "phrases" for "phases," and corrected to make the word read "pharses."

3. Du Camp, *Souvenirs*, II, 342.
4. Richard, *Littérature et sensation*, p. 182.
5. Durry, *op. cit.*, pp. 151, 154, and *passim*.

Selected Bibliography

PRIMARY SOURCES

Madame Bovary, Moeurs de province. Paris: Michel Lévy frères, 1857.

Madame Bovary. New translation by Francis Steegmuller. New York, Random House, 1957.

Salammbô. Paris: Michel Lévy frères, 1862. *Salammbô.* New translation from the French by Robert Goodyear and P. J. R. Wright. London: New English Library, 1962.

L'Education sentimentale, Histoire d'un jeune homme. Paris: Michel Lévy frères, 1869. *Sentimental Education, the Story of a Young Man.* Introduction by Louise Bogan. New York: New Directions, 1958.

La Tentation de Saint-Antoine. Paris: G. Charpentier, 1874. *Temptation of Saint Anthony.* Translated by Lafcadio Hearn. New York & London: Harper & Brothers, 1932.

Trois Contes. Paris: G. Charpentier, 1877. *Three Tales.* Translated. Introduction by Robert Baldwick. Baltimore: Penguin Books, 1961.

Bouvard et Pécuchet. Paris: Librairie Alphonse Lemerre, 1881. *Bouvard and Pécuchet.* Translated by T. W. Earp and G. W. Stonier. Introduction by Lionel Trilling. Norfolk, Conn.: New Directions, 1954.

Selected Letters. Translated, edited by Francis Steegmuller. New York: Farrar, Strauss and Young, 1957.

The most nearly complete edition of Flaubert's work is the *Oeuvres complètes de Gustave Flaubert.* Paris: Librairie Louis Conard, 1909-1953. 26 vols. Thirteen of these present the correspondence. Good critical editions of the novels are available in the *Classiques Garnier* series.

SECONDARY SOURCES

BRUNEAU, JEAN. *Les Débuts littéraires de Gustave Flaubert, 1831-1845.* Paris: Armand Colin, 1962. Thorough, up-to-date study of Flaubert's childhood and youth, and of the *Juvenilia,* this thesis replaces the pioneering work of Descharmes.

DUMESNIL, RENÉ. *Gustave Flaubert, l'homme et l'oeuvre.* 3rd ed. Paris: Desclée de Brouwer, 1947. This study, by the dean of Flaubert scholars, is out-of-date in places but still basic and indispensable.

GIRAUD, RAYMOND, ed. *Flaubert, a collection of critical essays.* Englewood Cliffs, N. J.: Prentice-Hall, Inc., 1964. Interesting appraisals by contemporary scholars and critics.

LEVIN, HARRY. *The Gates of Horn.* New York: Oxford University Press, 1963. Stimulating chapter on Flaubert.

RICHARD, JEAN-PIERRE. *Littérature et sensation.* Paris: Editions du Seuil, 1954. The essay on Flaubert is brilliant.

SPENCER, PHILIP. *Flaubert, a Biography.* London: Faber and Faber Ltd., 1952. Best full-length study in English.

SUFFEL, JACQUES. *Flaubert.* Paris: Editions universitaires, 1958. Brief, sound, up-to-date.

THIBAUDET, ALBERT. *Gustave Flaubert.* Paris: Gallimard, 1935. A great critical study.

Index

Index

71160

843.8
B922